DORSET
IN THE
WORLD WAR

Graham Smith

COUNTRYSIDE BOOKS
NEWBURY, BERKSHIRE

First published 1999
© Graham Smith 1999

COUNTRYSIDE BOOKS
3 Catherine Road
Newbury, Berkshire

ISBN 1 85306 586 2

To the fond memory of Jenny

The cover painting shows Typhoon 1bs of
No 181 squadron with invasion stripes over
the Dorset coast in 1944 and is reproduced
from an original by Colin Doggett

Designed by Mon Mohan

Produced through MRM Associates Ltd., Reading
Printed by Woolnough Bookbinding Ltd, Irthlingborough

CONTENTS

Dorset Airfields in the Second World War

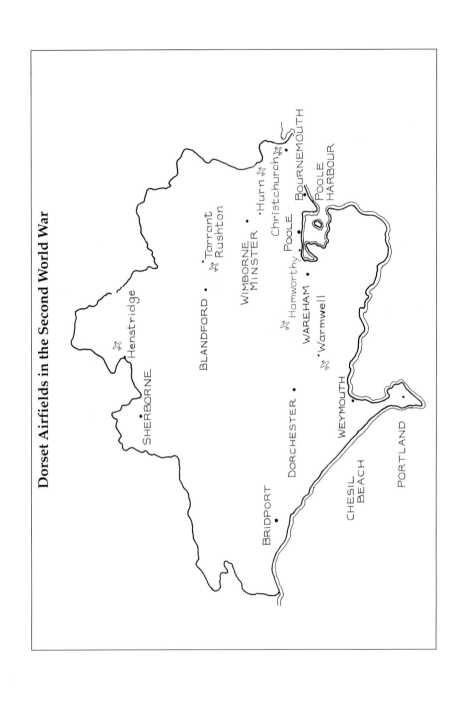

ACKNOWLEDGEMENTS

I am greatly indebted to a number of people for assisting me during the preparation of this book, especially with the provision of illustrations: Colin Cruddas and Mike Phipp were most generous in their help. Also my thanks to Jerry Shore of the Fleet Air Arm Museum, Christine Gregory of the RAF Museum, Sue Beckett of Poole Museum Service, Dawn Webster of the Priest's House Museum, Wimborne, and Mr E. Webber of the Sherborne Museum Association.

As usual I am grateful for the willing assistance of the staff of Galleywood Library of Essex Libraries Services for obtaining the many books used during my research.

Graham Smith

I

SETTING
THE SCENE

Dorset's long and proud history of aviation, both civil and military, can be traced back to the pioneering days of flying, a heritage to rival that of any other county. In 1910 Southbourne was the venue for what is considered the first international air meeting to be held in the United Kingdom, which was less than two years after the first recognised aeroplane flight in the country. The meeting attracted most of the celebrated aviators of the day, but sadly it made the newspaper headlines for another reason – the scene of the first fatal accident to an airman in the country. During the First World War the Royal Naval Air Service and the Royal Flying Corps were active in the county, and in the first year of peace Bournemouth played host to the later famous and prestigious Schneider Trophy race for seaplanes. The town could boast an aerodrome, said to be 'better suited to the joys of pleasure flying', at a time when very few cities could say the same.

During the inter-war period when the public's interest in flying seemed unbounded, many of the famous flying personalities of those exciting years could be seen at the various air shows and displays which were held throughout the county, and none was more prominent than Sir Alan Cobham and his Flying Circus. But it was with the outbreak of the Second World War, and the fall of France in June 1940, that Dorset was thrust into the frontline. Its situation on the edge of 'Churchill's

Moat' ensured that its handful of Service airfields were destined to play an important part in the air war, especially during two of the most vital periods – the Battle of Britain and Operation Overlord – the invasion of Europe.

In July 1910 an ambitious aviation meeting was planned as part of Bournemouth's centenary celebrations, and for the purpose a landing ground was prepared at Southbourne to the east of the town. Four pylons marked out the 3,140 yard course and a number of large canvas hangars were erected for the precious and fragile aeroplanes of the participants. The meeting duly opened on 11th July 1910 and was attended by several important visitors, including HRH Prince Arthur of Connaught, along with thousands of spectators, who were charged entrance fees of between 2s and 15s. With over £8,000 being available in prize money the meeting naturally attracted most of the country's leading pioneer aviators, as well as those from Europe and America – the first truly international meeting to be held in the country. Such famous names as Claude Grahame-White, Edmond Audermars, Colonel Samuel F. Cody, Leon Morane, J. Armstrong Drexel, the Hon C. S. Rolls, G. A. Barnes, and William McArdle (Bournemouth's first licensed pilot) participated in the various competitions, and even Louis Bleriot attended as a visitor, which made the meeting a veritable roll-call of early aviation history.

Grahame-White, who the following year would establish his own aerodrome and aircraft factory at Hendon, offered 'Sky rides' in his 'Autobus', when 'Mrs Astley and other ladies' took to the air; it would become fashionable for ladies to make at least one flight with a 'flying man'. It was reported that Grahame-White received over £1,300 from passenger fees and prizes whilst at Southbourne. J. Armstrong Drexel was the son of a wealthy Philadelphian banker, who seemed to specialise in high-altitude flying and would hold the world's height record (9,449 feet) in his Bleriot aeroplane on several occasions during 1910.

Unfortunately the Bournemouth meeting is now almost solely remembered for the fact that the Hon Charles Stewart Rolls was tragically killed on 12th July when his French-built Wright biplane suffered a structural failure in flight. Rolls was a founder member of both the Royal Aero Club and the Royal Automobile Club, and had, just a month earlier (2nd June), made the first flight from England to France

J. Armstrong Drexel at the Southbourne meeting in 1910.

and back without landing in France. This first fatal aviation accident is commemorated by a plaque in the grounds of St Peter's School, Southbourne.

During the First World War the Admiralty established a number of airship stations around the coast, of which three were sited in Dorset – Upton, Toller (or Powerstock) and Moreton – although the latter was never in fact used. From 1915 onwards 'SS' (Submarine Scout) type non-rigid airships, Class C (Coastal) and later 'SSZ' or 'Zero' airships patrolled the coastal seas looking for enemy submarines. These were commonly known as 'Blimps' and as one intrepid Naval airman later recalled, 'To fly a ship on a nice day was a really delightful experience. One felt that the air was entirely one's own.' Although the airships were later provided with bombs, there were no bomb racks or sights, and the bombs were normally hung over the side on pieces of string, which were cut with a knife to release them! The main object of the airship patrols was to sight enemy submarines or mines and then transmit the information back to the Navy's wireless-direction finding stations spread along the coasts. Two of the 'Zero' airships, SZ45 and SZ14, force-landed near Bridport in July and October 1918 respectively.

The Royal Flying Corps was formed on 13th May 1912. Just four days earlier, on the 9th, a piece of aviation history was made during the Naval Review off Portland when Lieutenant C. R. Samson became the first man ever to fly an aeroplane – a Short 538 biplane – from a moving ship. In 1915 the RFC contracted the Bournemouth Aviation Company to train British and Belgian pilots at its new aerodrome at Talbot Village, which was close to Winton and later became known as RFC Winton. It is interesting to note that the word 'aerodrome' is derived from the Greek and it literally translates as 'aerial racecourse'. The term was used for aircraft landing grounds well into the Second World War, before being universally replaced by the American derivative 'airfield', although the old term is still in current use in the private pilot's 'bible', *Pooley's Flight Guide*. In 1917 the Bournemouth Aviation Company moved to a larger site at Ensbury Park, about three miles to the north-west of Bournemouth, where elementary flying training continued for the rest of the war.

In September 1916 the Royal Naval Air Service, which until 1st July 1914 had been merely the Naval Wing of the RFC, set up a seaplane base at Portland between Chesil Beach and Portland Castle. No 241 squadron was formed at Portland initially with two flights and they were equipped with a number of Short 225 and 240 seaplanes for anti-submarine patrols along the English Channel. As the shore establishment developed and grew, it became known as HMS *Sereptia*, but in April 1918 with the formation of the Royal Air Force, it was transferred to the new Service and in June 1919 No 241 squadron was disbanded.

From 1916 onwards the RNAS had also established a number of small coastal aerodromes for use by short-range anti-submarine aircraft. One of these was sited at Chickerell, about 1½ miles to the north-west of Weymouth. Some 34 flights were equipped with de Havilland DH 6 patrol aircraft, which had been originally designed as two-seat elementary trainers and were produced by a number of aircraft companies. The DH 6 was never very inspiring either in appearance or apparently to fly, as it was variously nicknamed 'The Crab', 'The Clutching Hand' or 'The Flying Coffin'! In June 1918 'D' Flight of No 253 'Hyderabad' squadron from RNAS Bembridge on the Isle of Wight arrived with just three DH 6 patrol aircraft. Two months later they were

Airco DH 6 variously known as 'The Crab' or 'The Flying Coffin". (Fleet Air Arm Museum)

The 'Immortal 504' was a familar sight in the Dorset skies. (RAF Museum)

replaced by aircraft of No 513 Flight of No 241 squadron at Portland, though by the end of the year they, too, had departed. The small grassed airfield at Chickerell was used during the late 1920s as a temporary base for Fleet Air Arm aircraft engaged on exercises with naval vessels based at Portland, and the airfield would later play a minor role during the Second World War.

At the end of the war Ensbury Park returned again to civil use with the Bournemouth Aircraft Company operating a handful of Avro 504s. The aircraft dated back to 1913 and became known as the 'Immortal 504'. After sterling service in the First World War as a bomber, the 504 would become one of the classic trainers of all time, operating as such until replaced in 1933. This remarkable biplane had been produced in such numbers during the war that a vast number had survived. Many were purchased by private individuals, giving them their first experience of piloting and offering joy rides to the public. The Avro 504 was a familiar sight in the Dorset skies during the inter-war years, especially around Christchurch where one was used for pleasure flights.

The town's 'airport', as Ensbury Park was proudly described, became the arrival point for a regular weekend passenger service from Cricklewood in Middlesex. Handley Page Aircraft Ltd had, in April 1919, hastily converted four of its 0/400 heavy bombers (or 'bloody paralysers' as they were known in the war!) into passenger carrying aircraft. In the following month they were granted British Certificates of Airworthiness under the new Air Navigation Regulations, and on 5th June the first commercial passenger service was flown to Ensbury Park by Lieutenant Colonel W. F. Sholto-Douglas, the company's chief pilot, in an 0/400 aircraft with the civil registration letters – G-EAAE. Sholto-Douglas would later become the AOC-in-C of both Fighter and Coastal Commands during the Second World War. Because this new air service did not show any appreciable saving of time on the existing railway service, it only survived until the middle of August.

The aviation highlight of the first year of peace should have been the resumption of the Schneider International Seaplane competition, which would take place off Bournemouth on 10th September 1919. It is better known as the Schneider Trophy, from the bronze and marble statuette that had been donated by the French munitions heir Jacques Schneider. The race had been first staged at Monaco in 1913 and now the third race, organised by the Royal Aero Club, was to take place on a 20 nautical mile course from Bournemouth Pier to Swanage Bay, thence to Hengistbury Head and back, for a total of ten laps. Unfortunately a heavy sea mist turned the race into chaos and it was eventually declared null and void by the Royal Aero Club. However, the leading seaplane, a SIAI (Savoia) S.13 converted reconnaissance bomber flown by the Italian, Guido Janello, at an average speed of 107 mph, was later declared the winner after an appeal by the Italian team. This decision by the Royal Aero Club was later revoked by the Federation Aeronautique Internationale, but a compromise was reached to the whole sorry affair when Italy was given the right to hold the following year's race, which took place at Venice on 21st September.

The Bournemouth race was eventful, as far as British aviation interests were concerned, by the entry of a Supermarine Sea Lion, designed by R. J. Mitchell, who would later design the Spitfire. Sadly, the Sea Lion sunk but it was later recovered and is now on display in the Science Museum in London, one of three aircraft to be seen there that have positive links with Dorset.

The Ensbury aerodrome continued to operate throughout the 1920s with the first summer aviation meeting being held in August 1926, when Captain Geoffrey de Havilland, OBE, won the Private Club Handicap Race in his Gipsy Moth. In the following year there were a number of flying accidents at the aerodrome, the most serious being a mid-air collision in June, which resulted in the death of Major Laurence Openshaw, Westland's test pilot. As a result of the spate of accidents the country's premier and prestigious King's Air Race, which was due to take place at Ensbury Park that year, was transferred to another venue. Sadly, the aerodrome never appeared to recover from these incidents and it closed, finally to disappear under housing development.

Another aviation 'first' can be claimed by the county. In March 1927 Charles N. Longman, an ex-RAF airman, founded the Young Airman's League, which was open to boys between the ages of 13 to 15 years. They were taught the principles of flight and aircraft construction, and the League was run along similar lines to the Boy Scouts. This League rather anticipated the formation (in July 1938) of the Air Defence Cadet Corps, which in February 1941 became known as the Air Training Corps (ATC) with HM the King becoming its first Air Commandant-in-Chief. The ATC was called 'a broad highway into the Royal Air Force' and it became the nursery for RAF airmen right up to the present day.

Sir Alan Cobham, KBE, AFC. (Flight Refuelling Ltd via Colin Cruddas)

It was in 1929 that Sir Alan Cobham, KBE, AFC, the celebrated and intrepid airman famed for his pioneering long-distance flights, undertook a long and exhausting flying tour of the country in an attempt to persuade local authorities to establish their own aerodromes – his 'Municipal Aerodromes Scheme'. For 21 weeks between May and October 1929, Sir Alan visited no less than 110 cities and towns in his DH 61 Giant Moth ten-seat aircraft, G-AEEV, which he had named *Youth of Britain* (he offered free flights for schoolchildren). During this tour he identified a site at West Parley, then some miles to the east of Bournemouth, as an ideal place for an aerodrome, and in the following year recommended its development to the Bournemouth Council, but to no avail. Of course the site subsequently became RAF Hurn. This was Sir Alan's first direct interest in aviation matters in Dorset, the start of his long and personal involvement in the county.

Many of the small private aerodromes that opened during the early 1930s became recognised and approved as 'landing grounds' as a result of the active support of the Automobile Association. AA patrol men, who had been specially trained to handle aircraft, were present at most of the air shows and displays. As the early aircraft were rather prone to mechanical failure, and also a ready supply of petrol was often quite vital, the AA produced, in late 1932, a *Register of Aircraft Landing Grounds*, all of those listed said to be 'conveniently situated close to country hotels, with petrol being readily available from nearby AA approved garages.' In the original register, which was regularly updated, there are two listed for Dorset, one at Cemetery Farm beside the Salisbury road out of Blandford Forum, and the other to the south-east of Shaftesbury.

One new aerodrome that did not appear in the original AA Register, although it was later included, was the small landing ground of just 34 acres at Somerford Bridge near Christchurch. It had been used by Captain Francis C. Fisher since 1930, who offered pleasure flights in his Avro 504K – G-EBVL. In March 1934 he moved to a new site close to the River Mude, and soon Christchurch aerodrome began to figure in the timetables of various small airlines. In the following year Bournemouth Airport Ltd was formed, with Sir Alan Cobham as Chairman and Captain Fisher as Managing Director, to develop the aerodrome. In May Cobham Air Routes Ltd started a regular service from London to Guernsey via Portsmouth, Southampton and Bournemouth

(Christchurch). It was later sold to Olley Air Services. Over the next few years a number of small airlines would use Christchurch with varying success, and Bournemouth Flying Club with Captain Fisher as Chief Instructor offered flying instruction.

The fast growing popularity of flying during the early 1930s owes much to the drive and enthusiasm of Sir Alan Cobham; indeed, he later wrote that his life's work had been 'the development and promotion of aviation.' From April 1932 his so-called Air or Flying Circus, billed as the 'World's Greatest Air Pageant', travelled the length and breadth of the country with the intention of making Great Britain 'air minded'. On his National Aviation Days (later known as Displays) thousands of spectators were treated to aerobatic displays, spectacular stunt and 'crazy' flying, wing-walking and parachuting; but perhaps more importantly they were given the opportunity of taking to the air for the first time on 'joy rides'. In four years, at hundreds of different locations throughout the country, well over one million people experienced the joy and thrill of flying. Some were fortunate enough to fly with Sir Alan in his specially designed and produced Airspeed AS.4 Ferry, *Youth of Britain II*. From 1932 to 1935 the 'Circus' visited Bournemouth, Weymouth, Wimborne, Swanage, Bridport, Lyme Regis, Blandford, Gillingham, and Christchurch at least once and some venues more frequently, and it was estimated that over three million people paid to attend the air displays.

Despite the public's very apparent interest in flying there were still under 3,500 licensed pilots in the country, of whom only about 6% were women notwithstanding the intrepid and well publicised exploits of Amy Johnson, Jean Batten, Lady Bailey, the Duchess of Bedford *et al*, and the ladies' own flying competition – the Northesk Cup. It is interesting to note that Captain Fisher's wife, Iris Stewart, won this cup in July 1936 with a minimum amount of flying experience. The main reason for the small number of pilots was that flying was a rather exclusive and expensive pastime, which took it beyond the aspirations of most of the public. It was not until October 1938 that flying instruction was brought within the reach of the average man and woman with the establishment of the Civil Air Guard. For about £10 a member of the Civil Air Guard could obtain a full year's flying training. The response was quite amazing, with over 34,000 applying in the first two weeks, of whom some 4,000 were duly enrolled into the Guard. By July 1939 it was

Westland Wallaces flew from Warmwell in the pre-war years.

estimated that some 3,500 had obtained their pilot's 'A' licences by this means, although they had also been individually classified in categories 'related to their prospective value in war'! Many of these pilots would later serve with the RAF or in the Air Transport Auxiliary. Christchurch was one of the many aerodromes throughout the country where a unit of the Civil Air Guard was established.

Despite the RAF's large expansion programme during the late 1930s, there was just one new RAF airfield scheduled for completion in Dorset – Woodsford, later renamed Warmwell. The *raison d'être* for this new Service aerodrome was the presence of two aerial bombing/gunnery ranges at Chesil Beach. It opened in May 1937 as part of the Armament Training Group and would become the home of No 6 Armament Training Camp. The first aircraft arrived in July – Avro Tutors and Westland Wallaces – both biplanes, which had rather passed their sell-by dates and would operate as target-towers. The latter aircraft, which had first entered the Service in early 1933, had gained a certain fame when one was flown at a height of 31,000 feet over Mount Everest during the

Houston expedition in April 1933. The Wallace only operated in five squadrons with just over 100 produced. It remained as a target-tug until being finally 'retired' in August 1943. There is a full scale model of a Westland Wallace on display in the Science Museum.

Despite the long and critical battle that was to begin for air superiority over Europe, civil aviation, in the shape of British Overseas Airways Corporation (BOAC), still managed to survive and was able to operate overseas services both by land and by sea; its majestic flying boats regularly left Poole Harbour for America, India, Australia, Africa and Portugal. Then for an all too brief period immediately after the Second World War, Hurn airfield was the country's major international terminal for landplanes. BOAC continued to operate its long-distance flying boat services from Poole Harbour until March 1948. Christchurch, which since 1941 had produced, assembled and modified Service aircraft and Horsa gliders, continued into the early 1960s with Vampires, Sea Venoms and Sea Vixens. Its most famous post-war civil aircraft was the elegant and handsome AS.57 Ambassador airliner, which equipped British European Airways' 'Elizabethan' fleet from 1951. From 1948 onwards until it moved into Hurn in 1980, Sir Alan Cobham's Flight Refuelling Ltd operated from the redundant RAF Tarrant Rushton airfield.

At the outbreak of the war RAF Warmwell was still the home of No 6 ATC but in less than a year would become an important Spitfire station deeply engaged in the Battle of Britain. Christchurch was requisitioned by the Air Ministry in September 1939 and became more famously known for its Airspeed aircraft factory. During 1940/1 Hurn was constructed, originally as a fighter satellite station but it actually became a major base for the support squadrons of the airborne forces. In the following year military flying boats shared the facilities at Poole Harbour with BOAC, and in April 1943 Henstridge opened as a Fleet Air Arm flying training airfield. Although it is actually in Somerset (only just!), the airfield is included here because the southern part of the Royal Naval Air Station did encroach into Dorset. The last wartime airfield to become operational was Tarrant Rushton, between Blandford and Wimborne, which would solely be used by squadrons supporting the airborne forces. In 1944 in the prelude to Operation Overlord squadrons of the RAF's 2nd Tactical Air Force used both Hurn and Warmwell, before the United States Army Air Force in the guise of the Ninth Air

20

Force operated briefly from these two airfields and also from Christchurch.

In order to appreciate the vital contribution made by Dorset airfields during the Second World War, it is helpful to examine Fighter Command, the 2nd Tactical Air Force and the operations of the Ninth Air Force in more detail. Then, to provide a balance, the rather dramatic rise and fall of the Luftwaffe will be examined. I am well aware that all these subjects fully merit far more space than this book will allow, so the accounts will, of necessity, be relatively brief.

Fighter Command

When the young men of Fighter Command faced their sternest test during the summer of 1940, they were serving in an organisation that was barely four years old. Many could remember the time when they were just a minor part of the Air Defence of Great Britain, which then controlled all operations by bombers, fighters, anti-aircraft guns and searchlights. The Command had come into being on 14th July 1936 when the Service was reorganised into four separate and distinct functional Commands – Bomber, Coastal, Training and Fighter. Its headquarters was established at Bentley Priory, Stanmore, which had been purchased by the Air Ministry in 1926 for £25,000, and it became the headquarters of what was known as 'the Inland Area'.

On that historic day in July 1936 the Command's first Air Officer Commanding-in-Chief, Air Marshal Sir Hugh C. T. Dowding, arrived without any fuss or ceremony to begin the herculean task of developing the meagre and out-dated resources of his new Command into a force capable of defending the country against an enemy bombing offensive. Perhaps it might have been argued that Dowding was the most unlikely person to command the body of rather extrovert, and very young, pilots that manned his fighter squadrons. Although he had served as a pilot during the First World War, he was now aged 54 years and fast approaching retirement. Dowding was a rather aloof and austere man with a reputation for a difficult and abrasive manner. Indeed, he acquired the nickname 'Stuffy'! However, Dowding proved to be an ideal choice; he was a most able administrator with complete confidence in his subordinate commanders, and was dedicated in his support and

Air Chief Marshal Sir Hugh C. T. Dowding, KCB, CMG. AOC-in-C, Fighter Command 1936–40.

concern for the welfare of his pilots, who were dubbed 'Dowding's chicks' by Winston Churchill. Furthermore he was blessed with considerable foresight. Without doubt Dowding developed a very fine fighter force and established a sound and effective defensive system, which together ultimately won what was, perhaps, the most critical battle of the war, against the most powerful air force in the world – the Luftwaffe.

Prior to his new appointment Dowding had been involved in the Service's various research, supply and development programmes and had been instrumental in the early planning of the Hurricane, Spitfire and Defiant. But more importantly he had actively supported the new and revolutionary device known as RDF or Radio Direction Finding – known to the Germans as 'DeTe' from Decimeter Telegraphy. This early warning system could detect the range, bearing and altitude of aircraft approaching the coasts and it proved to be an important and critical factor in the Battle of Britain.

The RDF stations were just the first line of the Home Defence System, which was an intricate and very effective communications organisation. Once the enemy aircraft had passed over the coast, it was the responsibility of the Observer Corps (granted 'Royal' status in April 1941) to track the progress of the enemy formations. They were required to identify every aircraft, Allied or enemy, and estimate their speed, height and bearing. Ultimately there were 29 Observer Corps' Posts in Dorset under the control of No 9 Group at Yeovil, and later a ROC depôt was set up at the Royal Bath Hotel in Bournemouth. The information on enemy aircraft was passed directly to Command headquarters, where it was filtered for errors, and then sent to Group headquarters. It was here that the enemy forces and their bearings were closely plotted on a large-scale map and the Group Commander decided how many and which of his squadrons he would use to face the threat. The necessary information and orders were relayed to the Sector stations within the Group, where the Sector Controllers would plot the information and 'scramble' their squadrons for interception, and from then onwards they would directly control the fighter pilots in the air. Allied to this fighter control system were the anti-aircraft defences, the barrage balloon force and the searchlight command – all under the control of Dowding and Fighter Command.

On 1st August 1939 Fighter Command comprised 37 squadrons

Wreckage of Heinkel 111K Mk VA shot down over the Lammermuir Hills near Edinburgh on 28th October 1939. (via R. S. Finlay)

based at the airfields in the three Groups – Nos 11 to 13. Of these squadrons nine were equipped with Blenheims and Gladiators, not really considered prime frontline fighters. Dowding had originally set a target of 53 squadrons as the *minimum* number he required to provide an adequate defence of the country. Thus the Command was equipped with some 740 Hurricanes and Spitfires to be pitted against an estimated Luftwaffe force of perhaps 1,500 bombers and maybe 1,000 fighters. However, within days of the outbreak of the war, four squadrons of Hurricanes were sent out to France, followed before the end of the year by another two, and yet another two squadrons were effectively 'lost' in the disastrous Norway campaign.

This depletion of Dowding's slim resources, which accelerated during the first weeks of May 1940, caused him grave concern as he considered that France was 'a lost cause' and the defence of Britain was his primary and major task. He felt so strongly about the situation that he requested to appear before the War Cabinet to personally state his case for the retention of fighters in England. This unique and unconventional action proved successful, as Winston Churchill announced on 19th May that 'no more squadrons will leave this country whatever the need of France.' Almost one month later he would famously say, 'What General Weygand called the Battle of France is over. I expect that the Battle of Britain is about to begin. The whole fury and might of the enemy must soon be turned on us. . .'

It was on 16th October 1939 that the Command claimed their first victories of the war – two Junkers 88s – that were shot down into the sea off the Scottish coast. Twelve days later a Heinkel 111 was brought down near Edinburgh, the first German aircraft to fall on mainland Britain. These victories were claimed by pilots of two Auxiliary Air Force squadrons, Nos 602 and 603 – first blood to the so-called 'weekend pilots'! But it was the air battles over France, and especially Dunkirk, that brought Fighter Command its first severe test. From 10th May to 4th June the action was intense and during that period the Command lost over 430 aircraft (mostly Hurricanes). With fighter production now exceeding 400 per month, these losses, although heavy, were not overly serious; it was the loss of some 300 trained pilots, many of them experienced pre-war officers and men, that proved to be critical.

For most of the Battle of Britain it was the supply of trained pilots that caused the greatest concern to Dowding and for many weeks during the height of the Battle his pilot establishment was short by at least 13%. He devised a system of moving hard-pressed squadrons out of the front-line to enable his experienced pilots to obtain a short respite from almost continual combat and to train new replacement pilots. In late July he ordered that his pilots should have eight hours off duty in every 24, and a continuous 24 hours off duty each week. Dowding's almost paternal concern for his 'Dear Fighter Boys' is shown in his letter to them on 2nd June 1940:

I don't send out many congratulatory letters and signals, but I feel that I must take this occasion, when the intensive fighting in Northern France is for the time being over, to tell you how proud I am of you and the way in which you have fought since the "Blitzkrieg" started.

I wish I could have spent my time visiting you and hearing your accounts of the fighting, but I have occupied myself in working for you in other ways.

I want you to know that my thoughts are always with you, and that it is you and your fighting spirit which will crack the morale of the German Air Force, and preserve our Country through the trials which lie ahead.

Good luck to you

H.C.T. Dowding.
Air Chief Marshal

Despite the hectic air combats of the early days of July, the Battle of Britain officially started on 10th July and finished on 31st October 1940. At least, those were the dates for which the 'Battle of Britain Clasp' was awarded to all airmen (2,945) flying at least one operational sortie during those 114 momentous days. The Command had a total frontline strength of 56 squadrons with six of these being non-operational for various reasons. The majority were equipped with Hurricanes (29) and Spitfires (19), others with Blenheims or Defiants. Of the four Fighter Groups it was No 11 based at Uxbridge that would carry the heaviest burden. It covered London and the Home Counties along with part of East Anglia; but, of course, it could call on the immediate assistance of the squadrons based in the neighbouring Nos 10 and 12 Groups.

No 11 Group was commanded by a New Zealander, Air Vice-Marshal Keith Park, MC, DFC, who had been Dowding's right-hand man since 1936 and took over the vital post early in 1940. Park proved to be a highly effective and popular leader, and his calm, measured and careful tactics were to be most decisive during the Battle. His counterpart at No 12 Group, Air Vice-Marshal Trafford L. Leigh-Mallory, CB, DSO, had strongly differing views on the conduct of aerial warfare; he greatly favoured the use of fighter wings of three or more squadrons rather than operating just single squadrons. Leigh-Mallory, who had been in charge of the Group since 1937, was an energetic and popular commander, and bounded with self-confidence. He was vociferous in his criticism of Park and the use of his resources during the Battle; the 'Big Wing' controversy over the use of squadrons would greatly harm the reputations of both Dowding and Park after the Battle was over. Leigh-Mallory, however, later became head of Fighter Command, and ultimately was placed in charge of the Allied Expeditionary Air Force.

Until No 10 Group became operational on 8th July 1940, the West Country and South Wales had been under the control of No 11 Group. Air Vice-Marshal Sir Quintin Brand, KBE, DSO, MC, DFC, became its first Commander operating from Rudloe Manor, Box, in Wiltshire. Brand, who was South African by birth, had served with distinction in the Royal Flying Corps when as a Major he had commanded No 151, one of the first night-fighting squadrons, where he was known as 'Flossie' by his pilots! He had the rare distinction of destroying a Gotha bomber in the last raid on England of the First World War. In March 1920 he made the first flight to South Africa, after which he was knighted, and in the

Hurricane 1s practising intercepting a bomber. (Imperial War Museum)

immediate pre-war years he had been the Director of Repair & Maintenance at the Air Ministry. Brand was a very loyal and unswerving subordinate and colleague of Dowding and Park, especially in the 'post mortem' subsequently conducted into the Battle. He retired from the Service in 1943 and died in Rhodesia in 1968 aged 74 years. Ultimately his Group would contain 10½ squadrons operating from airfields at Middle Wallop, Warmwell, Boscombe Down, Pembrey, Exeter, St Eval, Bibury and Roborough. Up until 6th October the Group would mount some 8,300 sorties (17% of the total) and lose 116 aircraft in action or accidents, or 13% of the Command's losses.

Despite being greatly out-numbered the RAF pilots' one distinct advantage was that they were flying over their own homeland. Although many were shot down or crash landed, quite a number – almost 50% – managed to bale out safely, survive the ordeal and return to their squadrons to fly again. Whereas, the Luftwaffe pilots and crews had the disadvantage of flying over hostile territory as well as crossing the English Channel twice, often returning in badly damaged aircraft. The RAF pilots were exhorted not to pursue enemy aircraft over the sea, as the air/sea/rescue services were then in their infancy, although most ignored this order. They were constantly reminded that their main priority was 'the destruction of enemy bombers', and that combat against the enemy fighters was only a means to an end.

Both the Spitfires and Hurricanes had a considerable edge over the Luftwaffe's twin-engined fighter/bombers, the Messerschmitt Bf 110s, but on paper the performance of the Hurricane was slightly inferior to that of the single-engined Messerschmitt Bf 109, as indeed was the Spitfire at higher altitudes. Without doubt the Me 109 was a most formidable opponent for the RAF pilots, it was only hampered by its rather limited operational range. The initials 'Bf' stood for Bayerische Flugzeugwerke (Bavarian Aircraft Factory), and in 1938 Willy Messerschmitt acquired controlling shares in the company. The Me 109E (Emil) was the first to use the 'Me' prefix, but as German official documents show that both 'Me' and 'Bf' were used during the war, in this book the term 'Me' will be used.

It is possible, in retrospect, to divide the Battle into several separate phases. The first related to the Luftwaffe's attacks on Allied shipping in and around the Channel and east coast ports, which the Luftwaffe called 'Der Kanalkampf', as well as general fighter sweeps with the aim of drawing the RAF fighters into the air. This phase could be said to have lasted until 7th August. Then for the next two weeks or so the Luftwaffe concentrated on targets near the south coasts – airfields, RDF stations, aircraft factories and ports. From 24th August the Luftwaffe tended to attack targets as far as the London area with an all-out assault on fighter airfields mainly in No 11 Group. Air Vice-Marshal Park later maintained that, 'Had my fighter aerodromes been put out of action, the German Air Force would have won the Battle by 15th September.' But from 7th September the Luftwaffe changed tactics and proceeded to concentrate their forces on daylight raids directed against targets mainly in the London area, and the first night blitzes began. Daylight fighter/bomber operations continued well into the autumn, but by then the heavy night raids against London and other provincial cities were in full progress.

To summarise this intensive air battle, which continued almost unabated for over three months, is quite impossible in such a brief account. Three specific days do however stand out and proved to be

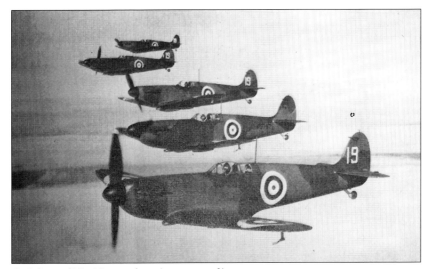

Spitfires of No 19 squadron in pre-war livery.

critical to the outcome of the Battle – 15th and 18th August, and 15th September – although it was on Sunday, 11th August that Fighter Command lost the most pilots in a single day, 25. However, it is important to note that in the many recorded accounts of the Battle, figures of losses on specific days do vary, even those taken from 'official' sources.

On 15th August the Luftwaffe lost 76 aircraft, their highest loss on a single day throughout the Battle, and it became known to its airmen as Black Thursday. Almost 2,000 sorties were directed at airfields and RDF stations along the south coast; some were flown from Norway and directed against targets in northern England. Fighter Command mounted 974 sorties and lost 35 aircraft with eleven pilots killed or missing in action. Three days later (the 18th), the day that the Luftwaffe was expected to defeat Fighter Command, huge Luftwaffe formations attacked RAF and Naval airfields, and as a result lost 67 aircraft compared with 33 RAF fighters destroyed. The day proved critical because the Luftwaffe had been convinced that Fighter Command was a spent force but the strength and ferocity of the opposition encountered made them realise that the battle for air superiority was far from won. As a result of this day's aerial battles Hitler was forced to postpone

Operation Sealion – the invasion of Britain – until 17th September; two days later Winston Churchill made his famous speech: 'Never in the field of human conflict was so much owed by so many to so few. . .'

By 15th September the Luftwaffe had turned its attention to daylight attacks on London. It launched some 1,000 sorties over London and in the process lost 61 aircraft (these figures were obtained from Luftwaffe records after the war). Fighter Command lost 31 fighters with 16 pilots killed, and the day was one of almost non-stop aerial combat. Some of the 'dog fights' took place over the centre of London to the great fascination of Londoners. The following day the Air Ministry claimed '175 Raiders Shot Down', which was later increased to 185 and Fighter Command's exploits were hailed as a historic victory, giving a massive boost to the public's morale. Hence the reason why the 15th September is celebrated as 'Battle of Britain Day'. The fact that this was based on grossly false figures really has little bearing on the matter. From then the German High Command fully realised that they could not gain air

1939–45 Star with a replica 'Battle of Britain Clasp'. (Spink & Son Ltd)

superiority over the English Channel and the planned invasion of Britain would again have to be postponed, as it was just two days later. As Winston Churchill later wrote of the day's fighting: 'It was one of the decisive battles of the war, and like the Battle of Waterloo, it was on a Sunday.'

Nevertheless the Battle continued, with each side incurring losses, especially during the last week of September, and not until the middle of November could it safely be said that the Battle of Britain was really over. On 30th September and 5th October two heavy German attacks were directed against the West Country, but these will be detailed later. Up to 6th October Fighter Command had lost over 900 aircraft against some 1,430 enemy aircraft destroyed. Although many experienced RAF pilots were lost during the Battle, a number survived and emerged as the outstanding fighter leaders and commanders of the war – 'Sailor' Malan, 'Al' Deere, Colin Grey, Peter Townsend, Brian Kingcombe, Donald Kingaby, Douglas Bader, 'Johnnie' Johnson *et al*. Surprisingly only one Victoria Cross was awarded during the Battle – on 16th August – to a Hurricane pilot, Flt/Lt J.B. Nicholson of No 249 squadron. It had been a hard, costly and narrow victory for Fighter Command, although by the end of November the two chief architects – Dowding and Park – had been relieved of their posts in favour of Air Marshal W. Sholto Douglas and Air Vice-Marshal T. L. Leigh-Mallory. At the time it seemed to be scant gratitude for their gruelling and valiant efforts. However, time has righted the balance and their somewhat tarnished reputations have been fully and rightly restored.

Until about the middle of the summer of 1941 the Command faced the difficult task of opposing the heavy night incursions of Luftwaffe bombers; in 135 major raids the Luftwaffe made 32,300 night sorties and lost 314 aircraft (0.97%). The Spitfires and, to a lesser extent, the Hurricanes were not really suited to night operations, but the Beaufighters, which had been hastily brought into service in September 1940, aided by the Defiants, did provide some opposition to the seemingly endless waves of enemy bombers. The Beaufighters, allied to AI (Airborne Interception), began to make some inroads into the Luftwaffe night bombers, especially in the hands of experts such as Flight Lieutenant John 'Cat's Eyes' Cunningham and his radar operator and navigator, Flight Sergeant C. F. Rawnsley.

Although the night defence of the country was still the Command's main priority, under its new Chief it began to move onto the offensive. On 20th December 1940 two Spitfires from Biggin Hill were sent out to strafe Le Touquet airfield and in the New Year the Command commenced a new operation, which went under the name of 'Circus', followed later in the year by other offensive operations variously known as 'Rhubarbs', 'Ramrods', 'Jim Crows', 'Rodeos' and 'Roadsteads'. These were a mixture of combined fighter operations with light or medium bombers, individual or squadron fighter sweeps to attack airfields and transportation targets in France and the Low Countries and anti-shipping strikes. With Air Vice-Marshal Leigh-Mallory now in charge of No 11 Group, his belief in the efficacy of 'Big Wings' resulted in the establishment of Wings at his various Sector airfields, although it was not until 1942 when greater resources were available and the improved marks of Spitfires had arrived that these Wings become really effective strike forces.

The Spitfires and Hurricanes were being refined and improved and with the provision of cannons were becoming quite formidable ground attack aircraft, the Hurricane being especially suited to this role. However, some of the operations were quite costly without showing really tangible results; during June and July 1941 there were 46 'Circus' operations mounted resulting in the loss of over 100 pilots including such famous Battle of Britain names as Bader, Mungo-Park and Lock. In the last six months of the year over 730 enemy aircraft were claimed to be destroyed for the loss of over 410 fighters. The actual figures turned out to be 154 enemy aircraft lost and not all these attributable to RAF action; a post-war study confirmed that each enemy aircraft destroyed lost the RAF 2.5 pilots! It seemed a poor return for some 75 squadrons then in operation. Now the tables were turned with Fighter Command operating over hostile territory with its pilots crossing the Channel. Also the new Me 109Fs appeared to hold the upper hand over the Spitfire Vs, and in September 1941 the Focke-Wulf Fw 190 made its first appearance. Its all-round performance proved to be superior to the Spitfire, a situation which caused the Command considerable problems until the Hawker Typhoon became more reliable and numerous, and superior marks of Spitfires were ultimately developed, notably the Mark IXs.

During 1942 the RAF suffered several set-backs. In February during the famous or infamous 'Channel Dash' of three German battleships,

Fighter Command launched 398 sorties, losing 17 aircraft without causing any serious damage to the German vessels, which managed to escape, although the Luftwaffe did lose the same number of aircraft. This fiasco was mainly due to a lack of planning and co-ordination between three operational Commands and the Royal Navy, and cast some doubt on the RAF's functional Command system. Two months later the onset of the so-called 'Baedeker' raids on cathedral cities and towns showed the vulnerability of the Home defences to this type of operation. From April to July Fighter Command accounted for 67 enemy aircraft, and of this number the newly arrived de Havilland Mosquito night-fighters claimed almost one third of the victories.

The biggest single task for the Command since the Battle of Britain came on 19th August with the ill-fated raid on Dieppe. During the day the Command mounted almost 2,400 sorties and claimed 96 enemy aircraft destroyed, another 39 probables and 135 damaged. It lost 91 aircraft (mostly Spitfires) and 47 pilots in the process but the press hailed the operation as a great victory because it was thought that over a third of the Luftwaffe's force on the Western Front had been destroyed or damaged. After the war it was disclosed that the 'real or actual' Luftwaffe losses were 48 destroyed and another 24 damaged; effectively a major defeat for Fighter Command, which would have caused the

Hawker Typhoon 1B of No 175 squadron, May 1943. (Imperial War Museum)

Command's chiefs very deep misgivings had they been aware of the true figures at the time.

In November 1942 a new Commander was appointed – Air Marshal Sir Trafford L. Leigh-Mallory – who was destined to command the force at the zenith of its power. By the end of the year the Luftwaffe had lost 244 aircraft in night raids, which at a loss rate of 10% was more than prohibitive. By the following June Fighter Command had doubled its size since the beginning of the war with a massive phalanx of fighters – Hurricanes, Spitfires, Beaufighters, Typhoons, Mosquitos and Mustangs. The new marks of Spitfires, especially, were proving themselves more than a match for the Luftwaffe fighters. Nevertheless, at the time, it gave the appearance of a large air force seeking a positive role in the European air war, and it has since been cogently argued that some of these vast resources would have been better employed by being diverted to the North African campaign and the Middle East. 'Rhubarb' sorties were being phased out and intruder raids and large fighter sweeps over France and the Low Countries had become the bread and butter of the squadrons, in addition to bomber escort duties, which greatly increased with the entry of the USAAF into Europe. By the end of the war over 11,000 intruder sorties had been made, accounting for over 500 enemy aircraft destroyed.

At the beginning of 1943 Fighter Command reached its peak with over 100 squadrons, of which three-quarters operated by day. It had become a most cosmopolitan force with the addition of Polish, Czech, Belgian, French, Norwegian, Canadian, Australian and New Zealand squadrons, making up about a third of the Command. Yet on 15th November 1943 the Command lost 32 of its squadrons to the Second Tactical Air Force. Even the name Fighter Command disappeared and in its place returned 'The Air Defence of Great Britain' – echoes of the early 1930s – which even at the time seemed a rather pointless and psychologically damaging decision. It was now commanded by Air Marshal Roderic M. Hill, CB, MC, AFC, who had previously been in charge of No 12 Group.

During January 1944 the remaining squadrons of the ADGB were faced with a new German night-bombing offensive mainly directed at London. On the 21st/22nd of the month the Luftwaffe launched Operation Steinbock in retaliation for Bomber Command's heavy raids on Berlin during the winter of 1943/4. However, by now the night defence squadrons were far better prepared and equipped. In the first

The first jet fighter to enter the Service – Gloster Meteor I. (RAF Museum)

raid 25 enemy aircraft were destroyed out of a total attacking force of
over 220. During the so-called 'Little' or 'Baby' blitz, the Luftwaffe
suffered heavily, losing over 240 aircraft mainly to the Mosquito night-
fighters.

In the two months leading up to Operation Overlord the ADGB flew
over 18,000 sorties and claimed 111 enemy aircraft destroyed for the loss
of 46 fighters. During D-Day its squadrons flew a total of 912 sorties,
mainly giving beach-head and shipping support as well as offensive
sweeps, and eight aircraft were lost. Further air support was given well
into July, although by that time its fighter squadrons were engaged in a
vastly different kind of air combat over London and Southern England.

The 'Baby Blitz' had brought such a crippling defeat for conventional
bombers, that German High Command was forced to turn to their
Vergeltunswaffe or 'Revenge weapons' – the V1 and V2 rockets – for a
last desperate bombardment of the country with London, East Anglia
and Southern England sustaining the brunt of the assault. Only one
week after D-Day (on the 13th) the first V1 rocket fell in Kent and from
then until almost the end of March a total of 9,251 V1s were plotted.

Twenty-two airmen are buried in Holy Trinity churchyard, Warmwell.

Perhaps at long last the fighter pilots had again found their true métier – single-handed combat – but this time against unmanned rockets or 'divers' as they knew them. In the whole V1 rocket campaign the RAF were credited with the destruction of 1,979; the most successful fighter at this type of combat was the Hawker Tempest with their pilots accounting for over 630. In August another new fighter was in action against the 'divers', the Gloster Meteor I, which became the first jet aircraft to see service in the RAF. Then on 8th September the first V2 rocket landed at Chiswick killing three civilians with another 17 seriously injured. These missiles, which travelled at a speed of more than 3,000 mph, were impossible to intercept, so fighter/bombers, especially Spitfire XIVs, were used to attack their launching sites.

On 15th October 1944 the Command regained its old and proud designation, with Air Vice-Marshal Sir Roderic Hill continuing as its AOC-in-C. Its squadrons were now deeply involved in escorting the massive daylight bombing operations which had become such a feature of Bomber Command's offensive over Germany. During March 1945 there were some isolated night intruder raids over eastern England with the object of attacking airfields as the bombers returned from operations. Notably on the night of the 3rd/4th the Luftwaffe mounted Operation Gisela, when over 140 night-fighters managed to destroy over

20 returning bombers with another three making crash landings. In the process the Luftwaffe lost over 20 aircraft, at least one third due to fuel shortages. The Luftwaffe's last incursion over England occurred on 10th April, the final death throes of what was once such a powerful air force. The final operation mounted by the Command during the Second World War was on 9th May when its squadrons provided air cover for the forces landing on Guernsey.

The men of Fighter Command could feel very proud of their valuable contribution to the air war. They had been called upon to carry out a multitude of tasks and in the process lost 3,690 airmen with 1,215 severely wounded and another 601 taken prisoner of war. Many of these brave airmen sacrificed their young lives, and are buried in the various country churchyards near to their old wartime airfields. Many more have no known graves and are suitably remembered at the very impressive RAF memorial at Cooper's Hill, Runnymede. Without doubt Fighter Command's greatest hour had been in those few brief months of the summer of 1940 when its young pilots held the fate of the country and the outcome of the war in their hands; for that Battle alone they should never be forgotten.

The 2nd Tactical Air Force

The formation of the 2nd Tactical Air Force on 1st June 1943 was thought, at the time, to be 'the most significant reform of the RAF since

Mitchell II of No 118 squadron.

37

the war began.' The decision to establish a Composite Group, which effectively became the nucleus of the new Air Force, was taken in early March, and its express purpose was to provide close tactical air support for the land forces that would be engaged in the assault on Hitler's 'Fortress Europe'. The target date for the invasion or Second Front, as it was generally known, was fixed for the following May at the Allied Trident conference in Washington; it was tentatively planned for 1st May 1944 but the Conference fully recognised that the imminent invasion of Sicily (in July) and the subsequent assault on mainland Italy might delay the starting date until June or even July. At this same conference the code-name 'Overlord' was chosen for the massive land, sea and air operation which became 'the largest and most complex single military operation the world had ever seen.'

The use of the title 'Tactical Air Force' followed naturally on from the example of the North-West African Tactical Air Force that had been formed in February 1943 specifically for the Tunisian campaign. But perhaps its most direct model in concept was that of the highly successful Western Desert Air Force, which had developed into a very mobile and efficient force, that had operated so closely and effectively with the Eighth Army to achieve almost complete air-land-sea co-ordination. Thus with effect from 1st June 1943 the Army Co-operation Command was dissolved and subsumed into the 2nd TAF. This new air force was orginally planned to comprise three operational Groups – Nos 2, 83 and 84 – which would, at least for the immediate future, be placed within Fighter Command under the nominal command of its AOC-in-C, Air Marshal Trafford L. Leigh-Mallory, KCB, DSO. This was purely a temporary expedient whilst Nos 83 and 84 Groups and their squadrons were being assembled, re-equipped and trained for their new roles. No 83 Group would operate with the 2nd British Army and No 84 in support of the 1st Canadian Army.

The 15 Army Co-operation squadrons, which were mainly equipped with Mustangs, along with the six Auster AOP (Air Observation Posts) squadrons, moved temporarily into Fighter Command. No 83 (Composite) Group had already begun forming on 1st April, whereas No 84 only began to take shape in June. It was officially formed at Cowley Barracks in Oxford, which was the headquarters of the British 2nd Army. No 2 Group of Bomber Command was transferred to 2nd TAF and into Fighter Command, on 1st June. Only five days earlier Air

Air Chief Marshal Sir Trafford L. Leigh-Mallory, KCB, DSO – AOC-in-C, Allied Expeditionary Air Force.

Vice-Marshal Basil Embry, DSO, DFC Bar, AFC, had taken over the command of the Group. He was probably the most able and forceful of all RAF wartime commanders, and an ideal choice for a tactical bomber strike force; at the time he was one of the few officers of Air rank that had wartime operational experience. His eight squadrons of light/medium bombers – Bostons, Venturas, and Mitchells – were passed over to Fighter Command, but Air Chief Marshal Harris, the Chief of Bomber Command, stubbornly refused to part with his two precious Mosquito squadrons. They were moved into No 8 (Pathfinder Force) Group.

Early in June, Air Vice-Marshal J. H. D'Albaic was provisionally appointed to command the 2nd TAF. He had been Embry's immediate predecessor at No 2 Group, but, during 1941, when D'Albaic had commanded the RAF forces in the ill-fated Greek campaign, he had voiced the opinion that 'the direct support to an army was not a proper use of air power'. This was certainly not a view that would sit too easily with the command of a Tactical Air Force, whose *raison d'être* was land forces support! In the event, by August 1943, at yet another major Allied conference – Quadrant held in Quebec – D'Albaic's appointment was not confirmed, and it would be another four months before the 2nd TAF's commander was finally appointed.

Perhaps the most important decision to emanate from the Quebec conference was the creation of another new Air Force, which would be called the Allied Expeditionary Air Force (AEAF) and composed of both RAF and USAAF components. Leigh-Mallory was appointed its Commander, mainly because it was envisaged that the prime role of the AEAF would be to provide fighter cover for the land troops, and Leigh-Mallory was the RAF's most experienced fighter commander. The AEAF would, in due course, be placed under the overall control of the Supreme Allied Commander, who had yet to be named and appointed. It was planned to be a massive air force, comprising some 11,400 aircraft – fighters, fighter/bombers, light bombers, reconnaissance aircraft and transports and glider-tugs for airborne troops – and it could be said that the AEAF would bear a certain close resemblance in composition to that of the all-conquering Luftwaffe in 1939/40.

The subsequent build-up of the RAF's 2nd TAF was rather slow and patient, but the squadrons of No 83 Group were soon in action, mostly engaged in fighter sweeps and reconnaissance patrols. A significant event occurred in June – the first operational use of rocket projectiles, ultimately the Force's most effective weapon. By the end of August over 5,000 sorties had been mounted by the Group, 200 tons of bombs dropped and 25 aircraft destroyed, but sadly for the loss of 35 pilots. In the following month almost the same number of sorties were flown and 14 enemy aircraft destroyed. The Group would eventually comprise over 50% Royal Canadian Air Force squadrons, and its pilots would claim their 100th enemy aircraft in January 1944. During this period of growth No 84 Group spent most of the time engaged in a number of land/air exercises of varying scales.

During the autumn of 1943 No 2 Group was re-equipping its Ventura squadrons with Mosquito FBVIs. This aircraft was, according to the Group's AOC, 'the finest aeroplane, without exception, that has been ever built in this country.' He had flown them operationally and was perhaps the most dedicated admirer of the 'wooden wonder'. On 3rd October they made a low-level attack on a number of transformer stations between Paris and Nantes, which Air Vice-Marshal Embry considered was the beginning of their operations under the aegis of the 2nd TAF. The Group's Mosquitos would launch a number of spectacular low-level precision raids over the next 18 months, perhaps none more daring than Operation Jericho in February 1944 – the attack on Amiens prison – and the several raids on Gestapo buildings in Holland and Denmark. However, during the winter of 1943/4 the Group's aircraft were mainly engaged in attacking V1 rocket sites in the Pas de Calais area of northern France and several on the Cherbourg peninsula. All of the Allied Air Forces were engaged in these operations, which had been code-named Crossbow; in fact, No 2 Group is credited with destroying 32 of the 80 sites that had initially been identified.

In early October 1943, No 38 Wing was upgraded to a Group and it would ultimately comprise ten squadrons of Stirlings, Halifaxes and Albemarles that would transport the airborne troops. A second Airborne and Transport Group, No 46, would later be formed with its five squadrons equipped with Dakotas (C-47s). The month also saw No 83 Group engaged in a major air/land troops exercise, Operation Limbo, to develop the logistics of working closely with an Army headquarters. The Allied air plans for Operation Overlord were now beginning to come together, with the USAAF's Ninth Air Force being re-activated in Britain as the American component of the AEAF, which was officially

Air Marshal Sir Arthur Coningham and Lieutenant General Lewis H. Brereton of the USAAF – the two Tactical Air Force Commanders.

Artist's impression of Hawker Typhoon 1Bs: these aircraft were the spearhead of 2TAF.

formed on 13th November. Two days later Fighter Command *per se* ceased to exist and in a much reduced state became the Air Defence of Great Britain. The following month No 85 (Base) Group was formed within the ADGB, with the objective of providing day and night fighter cover for the massive Allied land, sea and air forces gathering for the invasion.

There were still several major appointments to be made, and all went to those commanders who had been so successful in the Mediterranean. General Dwight D. Eisenhower was made the Supreme Allied Commander, and he recommended Air Chief Marshal Sir Arthur W. Tedder, GCB, to be his Deputy. Tedder was an officer with a wealth of command experience, who had been the C-in-C of the Allied Mediterranean Air Forces, where he had worked closely with both Eisenhower and General Montgomery, who was given the command of 21st Army Group, and made overall Commander of the Allied land forces for the initial phase of the invasion. Eisenhower later described Tedder as 'one of the few great military leaders of our time.' The final appointment was that of Air Marshal Sir Arthur Coningham, KCB, DSO, MC, DFC, AFC, as Commander of the 2nd TAF. Known as 'Mary' from 'Maori', which was a reference to his New Zealand origins, Coningham had a highly proven track record in army co-operation, first with the

Western Desert Air Force and later as Commander of the Allied North-West African TAF. In retrospect he seemed to be the obvious choice, and certainly under his inspired leadership the 2TAF became one of the greatest and most effective strike forces of the war. According to the *Official History of the RAF*, Leigh-Mallory delegated to Coningham, in April, the planning and operational control of both the British and American tactical air forces. Two other senior RAF commanders, who had also served with distinction in the Middle East, Air Vice-Marshals Harry Broadhurst and L.O. Brown, were given command of No 83 and 84 Groups respectively. The various commanders formally took up their new appointments in January 1944 so it could now be said that the greatest air offensive of the Second World War was about to begin.

As Leigh-Mallory later recorded, 'Next to air superiority the dislocation of the enemy lines of communications was the most important task set the Air Force. The basic intention was to force the

Typhoons of No 245 (Northern Rhodesia) squadron, No 121 Wing taking-off at dusk from Holmsley South. (Bournemouth International Airport via Mike Phipp)

44

enemy off the railways, initially within an area of 150 miles of Caen, to create a railway desert . . .' This offensive is probably better known as the Transportation Plan and was the brain-child of Professor Zuckerman, a senior scientific adviser on the staff of the AEAF, who had the strong support of Tedder. The Plan would require the employment of RAF Bomber Command and the USAAF's Eighth Air Force, and became the most hotly disputed and debated air offensive of all the pre-invasion air plans. This was mainly due to the strong possibility of heavy French civilian casualties and the firm opposition of both Air Chief Marshal Harris and Lieutenant General Carl A. Spaatz, who considered that their heavy bomber forces would be better deployed over Germany striking at industrial and, more especially, oil targets. The Transportation Plan was finally given almost reluctant approval, eighty major targets were identified, of which the AEAF was allocated 18, and to the eve of D-Day the AEAF mounted 8,736 sorties dropping over 10,000 bombs on railway marshalling yards, depots and junctions. Winston Churchill later wrote: 'The sealing off of the Normandy battlefield from reinforcements by rail may well have been the greatest contribution that the bomber forces could make to "Overlord".'

1st April can be considered the date when the various Allied air forces started their pre-invasion offensive in earnest. By that date most of the wings of Typhoon 1Bs, Spitfire XIs, Mustang IIIs, Boston IIIs, Mitchell IIs and Mosquito VIs of the 2nd TAF were in place at their various airfields and Advanced Landing Grounds in the southern counties. On the 8th of the month the first offensive sweeps were made by the Spitfire Wings,

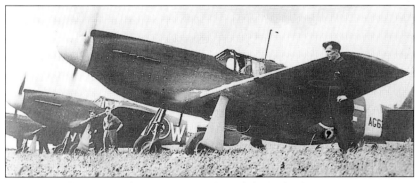

Mustangs of No 2 squadron in No 35 Wing of the 2nd TAF.

Spitfire LF IX 'AB196' was in No 308 (Polish) squadron of No 140 Wing.

followed twelve days later by the long-range Mustangs. In the period up to D-Day the Allied Expeditionary Air Force launched over 28,500 sorties, dropped almost 7,000 tons of bombs and in the process lost 133 aircraft. The ADGB squadrons operating under the Force's direction completed another 18,600 sorties, losing 46 aircraft but claiming 111 enemy aircraft destroyed.

The Force's targets were many and various – coastal batteries, radar and wireless transmitter stations, airfields, ammunition dumps, military depots, and road and rail bridges, particularly those crossing the Rivers Seine and Loire in an attempt to isolate the Normandy battleground. The Typhoon squadrons were highly successful in attacking the German radar stations along the Channel coast, with the result that by D-Day 76 out of 92 sites had been put out of action, and much of the coast was 'desolate of radar cover'. It should be noted that the air offensive was equally directed at the Pas de Calais in an attempt to confuse the enemy as to the exact landing area. From 21st May the Tactical Air Forces were authorised to attack trains and rolling stock, and on that day alone over 250 Typhoons, Spitfires and Tempests destroyed 67 locomotives. Another 1,388 sorties against locomotives would be made in the following two weeks.

By D-Day the 2nd TAF comprised over 100 squadrons of fighters, fighter/bombers, light bombers and transports; almost 3,000 aircraft. On the day the Force sent out over 2,200 aircraft to provide convoy and beach-head cover, close tactical air support, reconnaissance and artillery patrols as well as providing smoke-screen cover; 24 aircraft were lost. The two Airborne and Transports Groups made over 1,000 sorties and lost 20 aircraft. It was said that on D-Day 'the long neglected art of Army Co-operation reached its peak of effectiveness'. The Luftwaffe was able to fly just 319 sorties, less than a half were fighters, and in the process it lost 39 aircraft, such was the Allied air superiority, fully justifying General Eisenhower's message to his troops: 'do not worry about the aircraft above you because they will be ours'! By nightfall of D-Day No 83 Control Centre was ashore in Normandy and operating. On the following day the German Panzer Lehr armoured division was moving from Alençon into the battle area, when it was attacked by Typhoons, and over 130 lorries and tanks along with some 80 guns were destroyed; the first evidence of the potency of these strike aircraft. On the following day the Tempest Vs of No 150 Wing were engaged in their first air combat, and destroyed 4 Me 109Gs. By the 10th June No 144 (RCAF) Wing of Spitfires became the first RAF unit to operate from French soil (at Ste Croix-sur-Mer) since the dark days of May 1940.

From now on the 2nd TAF came into its own with its squadrons of fighter/bombers, armed with bombs, rocket projectiles and cannons, giving the infantry close air support in a most devastating manner. Anything that moved on the roads and railways by day came under fierce and intense attack. Field Marshal Rommel commented on 11th June: 'Our operations in Normandy are rendered exceptionally difficult

Mosquito FB VI of No 487 (RNZAF) squadron of No 140 Wing.

47

by the strong and in some respects overwhelming superiority of enemy air forces . . . [we] are bombed from the air with annihilating effect. Troops and staffs have to hide by day in areas with cover to avoid the constant attacks from the air.' Indeed, six days later the Field Marshal was severely wounded when his staff car was strafed by Spitfires.

By the end of June 1944 at least 38 squadrons were operating from Advanced Landing Grounds and in the first week of August most of No 84 Group moved over to France. Ultimately there were 31 emergency landing strips in the British zone of operations. The so-called 'cab-rank' system for the ground control of the fighters/bombers in frontline areas was introduced, similar to that used successfully in Tunisia. However, it had now been refined with the addition of armoured 'contact cars' operating in the frontline to locate enemy targets and then rapidly calling in, by radio, an instant and seemingly constant stream of Typhoons, Spitfires and Mustangs.

One of the most impressive demonstrations of the Force's destructive power came on 7th August at Mortain when some 400 tanks of six Panzer divisions, escorted by about 300 Luftwaffe fighters, threatened to cut off the US Third Army. The Luftwaffe fighters were engaged by fighters from the Ninth Air Force, allowing Typhoons of 2nd TAF a free hand to attack the armoured columns and to create utter mayhem. The squadrons operated a 'shuttle service' of attacking formations, mainly in pairs, and as the day developed, 'it was obvious that air history was being made', in the words of Air Marshal Coningham. The end result was a massacre, with the enemy retreating in complete disorder. The day's actions proved conclusively that a Tactical Air Force could be a most decisive factor in the land operations.

Perhaps an even more convincing confirmation of the devastating effect of concentrated tactical air power was shown about two weeks later in what has become known as the 'Falaise Gap'. The entrapped German troops and armour suffered for ten days a quite awesome and sustained bombardment from the fighter/bombers and fighters of the two Tactical Air Forces, which turned the German retreat into an utter rout. According to Wing Commander (later Air Vice-Marshal) J.E. 'Johnnie' Johnson, DSO 2 Bars, DFC Bar, who commanded three different Spitfire Wings of the 2nd TAF, it was 'one of the greatest killing-grounds of the war.' This effectively ended the Battle of Normandy, and it had been an outstanding triumph of air power. As Field-Marshal von

48

Hawker Tempest V of No 486 (RNZAF) squadron, one of the two Tempest squadrons to operate on D-Day with No 150 Wing. (via J. Adams)

Kluge, the German Commander-in-Chief, wrote to Hitler, 'There is no way by which, in the face of the enemy air forces' complete command of the air, we can discover a form of strategy that will counter balance its annihilating effect unless we withdraw from the battlefield.' The complete and utter victory in the air had not been without its cost. From D-Day until 31st August the 2nd TAF and ADGB had flown over 151,000 sorties and had lost 829 aircraft (mainly to flak) along with 1,035 aircrew killed or missing in action. In the same period the Luftwaffe had lost over 1,400 aircraft.

With the 2nd TAF now largely operating from airfields in France, it passes out of the scope of this account. However, it should be mentioned that the Force's operations against the defences of Calais enabled the Canadian troops to capture the German garrison of some 10,000-strong for the loss of 300 men. The 2TAF's Wings followed the Allied Armies' speedy advance across France and into Holland. Air Marshal Coningham, who on 14th September had set up his headquarters in Brussels alongside the 21st Army Group, had some 1,800 aircraft and over 100,000 airmen under his command, and hardly a day passed when his squadrons were not in action. In 1944 his air force had mounted over 20,000 operations, in which 38,000 tons of bombs had been dropped and over 130,000 rocket projectiles fired.

The only real set-back experienced by the 2nd TAF during its service on the Continent occurred on New Year's Day, 1945. This day saw the Luftwaffe's final and despairing major attack. The German High Command had managed to gather together a fighter/bomber force of 750 to 800 aircraft, which were mainly manned by inexperienced pilots and crews culled from training units, but they were led by experienced navigators in Junkers 88s. The operation known as 'Bodenplatte' or 'Baseplate' was a carefully planned and undetected low-level attack on the crowded airfields in the Low Countries and Eastern France, where the aircraft were parked wing-tip to wing-tip. The precise figures of RAF aircraft destroyed or written-off are not too clear, but they were possibly in excess of 150 with 40 airmen killed on the ground. But the Luftwaffe probably lost over 220, and some of these fell to their own flak batteries when returning to their German bases. The operation further weakened an already depleted Luftwaffe, while to the Allies it was a rather sobering check to their all-conquering progress so far, and had been mainly occasioned by over-confidence and complacency. With the Allied's production of aircraft totalling some 10,000 per month, the losses sustained were infinitesimal.

The last major operation for the 2nd TAF came on 29th April 1945 with Operation Enterprise – the crossing of the Elbe – when Tempests of No 122 Wing were in action, claiming 14 enemy aircraft, as well as destroying over 100 vehicles. The Hawker Tempest was essentially a Typhoon with a number of aerodynamic improvements. The aircraft had entered the Service in January 1944, and in the summer it made its mark against the V1 rockets, destroying well over 600. The Tempest V was one of the fastest fighters of the war, and proved quite a match for the Luftwaffe's Me 262 turbojets, destroying at least 20 in the final months of the war when the 2nd TAF had seven squadrons of these lethal fighters. Now occupying airfields in Germany that had not long ago been the pride of the Luftwaffe, No 83 Group was responsible for the air space to the east of the Rhine, and No 84 to the west. The Typhoon and Tempest squadrons were engaged in attacking shipping in the Baltic, with the 4th of May being the last operational day of the 2TAF. In the first four days of the month the 2TAF had destroyed over 140 enemy aircraft for the loss of 29 aircraft. The last Luftwaffe aircraft to be shot down by the RAF in Europe fell to Spitfire XIVs of No 125 Wing on 5th May.

Without a shadow of doubt the 2nd Tactical Air Force, along with the USAAF's Ninth Air Force, had clearly shown the formidable and destructive effect of strike aircraft operating in close tactical support of land forces. Since D-Day the two Groups had flown over 233,000 sorties, destroyed at least 1,450 enemy aircraft and had fired some 220,000 rocket projectiles. On 15th July the 2TAF ceased to exist and many of its squadrons became the nucleus of the post-war British Air Forces of Occupation in Germany. It has since been described as 'one of the greatest fighting units of the British armed forces', so it was not too surprising that the British Air Forces of Occupation in Germany was, in September 1951, renamed the 2nd Tactical Air Force. Its motto, 'Keepers of the Peace', reflected its changed peacetime role.

United States Army Air Force

During the Second World War the United States Army Air Force was present in Britain in great numbers, but the name that immediately springs to mind is that of the Eighth Air Force, known as the 'Mighty Eighth', with its massive and thunderous array of heavy bombers – B-17s (Flying Fortresses) and B-24s (Liberators) – along with their escort fighters, P-38s (Lightnings), P-47s (Thunderbolts) and P-51s (Mustangs). The first units of this major Air Force arrived in Britain in the summer of 1942 to join RAF Bomber Command in the Allied strategic bombing offensive, but they operated solely by day. Like its RAF counterpart the actions and feats of the Eighth Air Force are many and legendary, and the Eighth richly earned its sobriquet of 'Mighty' not solely on account of its size but also by the nature of its deeds. However, in late 1943 the Eighth was joined in Britain by a second American Air Force – the Ninth. During the Ninth's brief time in Britain, less than twelve months, it was rather overshadowed by its 'big brother', but it, too, grew into a large air force in its own right, and made an important and considerable contribution to the Allied tactical air offensive during the last 18 months of the war.

The origins of the Ninth Air Force can be traced back to 1941, before the United States of America entered into the Second World War, when a

B-26 Flak Bait of 322nd Bomb Group, 99th Bomb Wing. This aircraft completed over 200 missions. (Smithsonian Institution)

body known as V Air Support Command was first formed. In April 1942 this Command was renamed the Ninth Air Force, and it was sent for service in Egypt in the autumn of that year, with its first operations commencing in November. The Ninth's various operational units had been engaged in the battles over the Libyan desert and in Tunisia, as well as supporting the invasions of Sicily and mainland Italy. However, it was decided that the Ninth would become the American tactical air force for the invasion of Europe corresponding closely to the RAF's 2nd Tactical Air Force. The Ninth was effectively disbanded and then re-activated in the United Kingdom on 16th October 1943 with its headquarters at Sunninghill Park, Berkshire, to become the American element of the Allied Expeditionary Air Force.

Its commander was Lieutenant General Lewis H. Brereton, an ex-World War I pilot who had served in France. Brereton had gained a vast experience of the principles of ground-air support during the Ninth's service in the Mediterranean, and he was a dedicated apostle of the

All three American fighters of the Second World War can be seen in this photograph. (Smithsonian Institution)

creed of army co-operation. Furthermore he had already worked closely with and alongside such RAF commanders as Tedder and Coningham, who would join him in Britain during the build-up to D-Day. Brereton appreciated that his Air Force's main priorities should be to gain and hold air superiority, to disrupt enemy lines of communication, and to destroy enemy forces at the frontline in close co-operation with the troops on the ground. But when asked to sum up the ethos of his Force, Brereton answered simply with just one word – 'mobility'. Much of the Ninth's success in the prelude to D-Day, and for several months afterwards, was due to his strong and firm leadership, his wide operational experience and his undoubted abilities as a tactitian.

Initially the Ninth Air Force composed three operational Commands – Bomber, Fighter and Troop Carrier – with a Service Command to maintain and service what would very rapidly become a large Tactical Air Force. The build-up of the Ninth had, of necessity, to be very swift, and for this purpose over 100 units of the Eighth Air Force were

Major James H. Howard of 356th Fighter Squadron, Ninth Air Force, was awarded the Medal of Honor in January 1944. (Smithsonian Institution)

transferred to the Ninth, along with some 30 of its airfields in Britain. During 1944 units of the Ninth would occupy, if only for brief periods, 62 airfields or Advanced Landing Grounds in England before moving over to the Continent.

The saying 'From little acorns do big oaks grow' was very appropriate for the Ninth Air Force. In October 1943 it comprised just four operational Groups and less than 300 aircraft, but by May 1945 the Ninth had 45 operational Groups, with some 4,600 aircraft and over 200,000 personnel! The Ninth Bomber Command was re-activated in Great Britain during October when four Eighth Air Force Groups, operating B-26 (Marauder) medium bombers from airfields in Essex, were transferred to the Ninth; Major General Samuel B. Anderson was its first commander. His Command ultimately grew to eleven Groups (45 squadrons), including three Groups operating A-20 (Havoc) light bombers. The Ninth's Fighter Command, which was slower in growth, became active in November under the command of Major General Elwood R. 'Pete' Quesada, who would prove to be a quite outstanding fighter commander. The first few Fighter Groups began to arrive in November, and they would also operate initially from airfields in East Anglia. They brought the first P-51s to serve in the USAAF. At this time

A-20G with Invasion Stripes over the English Channel on D-Day. (USAF)

the aircraft was considered by Washington to be a tactical support fighter, rather than the superb long-range 'pursuit' fighter that it finally became. The Fighter Command would ultimately comprise 18 Groups (54 squadrons), in addition to two Tactical and Photo Reconnaissance Groups and a couple of night-fighter squadrons.

In April 1944 the Command would devolve into two 'Tactical Air Commands' – the 9th and 19th – recognising the slightly different roles they would play in Operation Overlord. It was commanded by Major General Otto P. Weyland, another fine tactical commander, who would go on to command the Ninth Air Force from 23rd May 1945. The three major American fighters of the Second World War operated in the Ninth, but perhaps none more successfully than the rugged and powerful P-47, which really found its true métier operating in a fighter/bomber role. The Ninth's Troop Carrier Command finally totalled 57 squadrons of C-47s (Dakotas) and C-53s (Skytrains), which would see action in the three major airborne troop operations of the war – D-Day, Arnhem and the Crossing of the Rhine. The Ninth also had a number of Engineer Battalions (Aviation), many of which landed as soon as the Normandy beach-heads had been secured in order to construct the first Advanced Landing Grounds in France. Ultimately these engineers constructed 50 such airfields.

From late 1943 the Ninth's bombers from their Essex airfields were heavily engaged in attacking V1 rocket sites, enemy airfields, railway marshalling yards and other strategic targets in France and the Low Countries. These operations were conducted with very light losses, at least compared with the Eighth Air Force's heavy bomber losses. The B-26s, which had started the war with such a wretched and unfortunate reputation, became one of the shining successes of the Ninth Air Force, and few USAAF chiefs would have predicted such a fine operational record for these rather vilified medium bombers.

In the early months the Ninth's fighters were mainly used as escorts for the Eighth's B-17s and B-24s on their heavy bombing operations. One P-51 pilot memorably recalled that right up to May 1944 'we were acting as nursemaids to our big brothers'! In January 1944, Major James H. Howard of 356th squadron of the Ninth's 354th Fighter Group operating from Boxted in Essex was awarded the Congressional Medal of Honor (equivalent to the Victoria Cross) for his brave actions in single-handedly saving B-17s of 401st Bomb Group from decimation whilst on

A-26 'Invader' of 386th Bomb Group. A-26s were introduced into the Ninth
Air Force in the summer of 1944. (USAF)

a mission to Oschersleben. His amazing and bravura performance,
which lasted for about half an hour, was later described as 'like
something out of a Hollywood film . . . one lone American against what
seemed to be the entire Luftwaffe.' Major Howard would be the only
American fighter pilot to receive this highest bravery award throughout
the air war in Europe.

By March the Ninth Bomber Command was able to direct its attention
towards tactical targets in support of the coming invasion. During the
month over 4,000 sorties were mounted and over 5,000 tons of bombs
dropped on railway centres, rocket sites, airfields and shipping targets,
for the loss of only eleven aircraft. Also in the month the number of
Fighter Groups had increased to seven and their main activity still
remained as escort support for the Eighth Air Force, but the first dive-
bombing operations by P-47s were carried out. Towards the end of the
month P-51s were authorised to undertake low-level attacks on railway
targets and airfields, the first being launched on 26th to Criel marshalling
yards and airfield. On the 20th of the month the Ninth mounted a major
mobility exercise, to practise what would happen when its Groups
would be operating from airfields on the Continent. The Ninth's ethos
was captured by the slogan of this exercise, 'Keep Mobile'!

C-47s & C.G.-4 Gliders of Ninth Troop Carrier Command lined-up, 7th June 1944. (National Archives & Records Administration)

From 1st April until the eve of D-Day the Ninth Air Force made 53,800 sorties, dropped 30,700 bombs and lost just under 200 aircraft in the various operations; this was the highest number of sorties undertaken by any of the Allied air forces engaged in Operation Overlord. The Ninth had been allocated 21 targets under the Transportation Plan, and they ranged from Aerschot to Valenciennes. Like their British colleagues in the 2nd TAF, airfields, rail and road targets, coastal batteries and bridges were attacked by both the light/medium bombers and fighter/bombers. Of the 24 rail and road bridges over the River Seine between Paris and Rouen the Ninth destroyed 18; the 'bridge-busting' prowess of the Ninth became legendary and this type of operation would continue well into August.

The B-26s proved to be ideal for these operations. They usually made the initial attacks, followed closely by the rugged P-47s dive-bombing with great accuracy. It was fully recognised that bridges were not the easiest targets to hit, and furthermore they were usually well defended by heavy and light flak batteries. Indeed, on 9th August Captain Darrell R. Lindsey of 394th Bomb Group was posthumously awarded the

Congressional Medal of Honor for his brave actions whilst bombing a rail/road bridge over the River Seine at L'Isle Adam. Almost invariably the bridges required further attention as the Germans seemed to be particularly adept at making hasty repairs. A close analysis of the bridge attacks, which was made after the war, revealed that 600 tons of bombs were required to ensure a bridge was destroyed by heavy bombers compared with 160/200 tons by medium and fighter/bombers. The attacks on enemy airfields also became one of the Ninth's specialities. It had been allocated 36 ranging from Brittany to Holland, and during this period 56 separate attacks were made with over 3,100 bombs dropped.

Like the 2nd TAF the Ninth's fighter/bombers were given *carte-blanche* to attack the enemy's locomotives and rolling stock, which had hitherto been proscribed because of the risk of heavy French civilian casualties. This embargo had been lifted because the French railway system was now almost solely used for the transport of German troops and supplies. The first day of this new offensive, 21st May, became known in the USAAF as 'Chattanooga Choo-Choo' from the popular song of the time. Both the P-47s and P-51s became most effective in 'loco-busting', as the American airmen called these strikes; the numbers of engines and rail wagons destroyed and damaged slowly mounted over the two weeks, causing considerable disruption to the French railway system.

In the weeks before D-Day the pilots of the Ninth Photo Reconnaissance units, flying F-5Bs (converted P-38s), were very active producing excellent low-level photographs of the coastal and beach defences, as well as the terrain further inland, building up a valuable

P-61 'Black Widow' night-fighter at Hurn – summer 1944. (USAF)

photographic archive of the land that would be the battleground in the vital months ahead. The 10th Photo Reconnaissance Group operating from Chalgrove, would receive a Distinguished Unit Citation for its operations over this period. The USAAF reserved this highly prized award for a Group's meritorious performance on a single mission or a succession of operations. They were, of course, greatly valued by the Group's personnel and were formally presented with full military ceremony.

By the evening of 5th June all Allied aircraft engaged in Operation Overlord were painted with the invasion stripes of alternating black and white bands around the fuselages and wings, ready for the big day. At American bases this was known as the 'Cake Walk', so called because it was said that for security reasons that was the name shown on the labels of the paint tins! Lieutenant General Brereton had over 3,500 bombers, fighter/bombers, and fighters under his command. The first Ninth Air Force aircraft to go into action on D-Day were the 14 Groups of the Troop Carrier Command, who delivered the men of 82nd and 101st Airborne Divisions. Of the 821 transports sent, 805 reached the dropping zones and 21 were lost. The Ninth's bombers were given the task of attacking the three coastal batteries and seven beach defences guarding the Utah beach-head. The B-26s and A-20s were forced to attack at a height of 3,500 feet because of the low cloud, and it proved to be one of the more successful daylight operations mounted on the day. The P-38s were placed on convoy air cover, with the other fighters and fighter/bombers giving cover over the beach-head as well as attacking targets immediately behind Utah, where the US 4th Infantry Division would land. Over 3,300 sorties were flown, 1,825 tons of bombs dropped, 22 aircraft lost and 5 enemy aircraft claimed to have been destroyed. For the rest of the month some 40,000 sorties were flown by the Ninth and over 200 aircraft were lost, mostly to flak.

Up until 23rd June the Ninth's medium bombers had been largely used in attacks on bridges, but now their attention was turned once again to V1 rocket sites, along with the other Allied air forces. Towards the end of the month the first units of the Ninth moved across the Channel, and on 22nd they made their first all-out attacks on the defences of Cherbourg. The so-called 'Great Storm' of 20th June, which had caused havoc with the massive programme of supplying the Allied armies in the field, made the capture of the port of Cherbourg a priority.

Enemy strongholds and troop concentrations in the Contentin peninsula finally capitulated under the heavy and concentrated attacks of the Ninth's fighter/bombers and bombers.

In the following month some of the Bomber Groups moved out of their Essex airfields into Hampshire, merely the first step towards operating in France. Although bridges still figured large in the Ninth's bombing schedules, its Groups were engaged in two operations that showed the effectiveness of tactical air support. In the middle of the month they were engaged (along with the 2nd TAF) in the Battle of Caen, wherein Caen and the surrounding area suffered the full weight of all the Allied air forces, which was described as the 'greatest bombing concentration of the war so far'. On the 25th of the month Operation Cobra was launched, the now famous offensive of the American 1st and 3rd Armies, which resulted in the successful break-out from St Lô. In seven days the Ninth Tactical Air Command mounted over 9,000 fighter/bomber sorties, a shattering demonstration of the use of air power in support of ground troops. One German officer later recalled, 'It was hell . . . the planes kept coming overhead like a conveyor belt.'

In August the Ninth Air Force had a change of Commander-in-Chief, when General Brereton somewhat reluctantly handed over the reins to his deputy, Major General Hoyt S. Vandenburg. Brereton had been selected to command the newly formed First Allied Airborne Army, which would first see action in Operation Market Garden – the Arnhem airborne landings. The Ninth Bomber Command was also re-designated the Ninth Bombardment Division and would remain so for the rest of the war. During the month the Ninth's units were engaged in the 'Falaise Gap' battle, although bridges still remained frequent targets. Perhaps one of the most successful days came on the 25th of the month – the day Paris was formally surrendered; the 19th TAC had played no small part in the the American advance on Paris. On this day three Fighter Groups won DUCs for their actions in accounting for over 110 enemy aircraft in the air and on the ground.

In the last week of August the American Lieutenant General Omar N. Bradley had requested an all-out air offensive against Brest and the surrounding defences, to soften up the German forces that were stubbornly resisting the US ground troops in Brittany. It was decided that the Ninth should accord these targets a very high priority. The 'Battle of Brest' became an almost separate campaign in its own right, as the main battlefronts moved further and further eastwards. The area became known to the Ninth's aircrews as 'the Brest Bombing Range' because of the frequency of their attacks and the relatively light flak opposition they encountered. For 23 days Brest and the surrounding area suffered the full weight of the Ninth's bombers and fighter/bombers, with over 5,700 sorties being launched before Brest finally fell to American troops on 19th September, when much of the town and port had been quite devastated. It has since been argued that these operations were a waste of valuable resources and could have been better employed supporting the main Allied armies as they moved steadily eastwards across France and into the Low Countries. It was during these operations that the Ninth introduced a new medium bomber into operations – the Douglas A-26 (Invader) – which was the last American 'attack or strike' aircraft to be developed during the war. It was intended to replace both the B-26 and A-20, and came into greater use in the final months of the war. By the end of the war some 1,500 Invaders had been built, and when the B-26s were finally phased out, the Invader was re-designated B-26 and operated successfully in the Korean War.

By the end of the month all of the Ninth's fighter/bomber and bomber Groups were operating from airfields in France, and they also pass out of the purlieu of this account. Like the 2nd TAF the Ninth followed in the wake of the Allied armies across France, into Belgium and Holland before finally crossing into Germany; its Groups moved airfields or landing grounds very frequently, fully justifying General Brereton's original concept of a 'mobile air force'. The Ninth's Groups fought with distinction and bravery during the enemy's counter-offensive in the Ardennes in late December 1944 (as indeed did the 2nd TAF). Several of the Bomber and Fighter Groups gained Distinguished Unit Citations for their actions, in what was better known to the Americans as the 'Battle of the Bulge'. Like the 2nd TAF the Ninth also suffered at the hands of the Luftwaffe on New Year's Day in Operation Baseplate, and almost 80 American aircraft were destroyed or damaged, including a number of Eighth Air Force fighters that were operating on escort duties from these Continental airfields.

In the last two weeks of the war the Ninth's units flew over 4,400 operational sorties, losing over 180 aircraft, mainly fighter/bombers. The Ninth Bombardment Division mounted its final operation on 3rd

May to targets in Czechoslovakia, with the fighters and fighter/bombers still in action on 8th May. The Ninth's relatively short war record in the European Theater was most impressive and highly commendable. Some 368,000 sorties had been made for the loss of 2,944 aircraft (over 70% were fighters) and 3,439 airmen were either killed or missing in action; but 4,186 enemy aircraft were destroyed in the air with another 365 on the ground. In his valedictory message to his men Lieutenant General Vandenburg acknowledged the 'evidence of the tremendous role of air power in accomplishing this historic success. . . Each man who fought and died is inseparable with those who fought and lived. . . To each one of you is due this credit. Our force could not have fought without the untiring effort of the individual. . .' Many of the Ninth's Groups were soon on their way back to the USA, although a number remained in Europe assisting with the Occupation. Finally the Ninth was 'de-activated' on 2nd December 1945; many of its airmen who flew from these shores, never to return, are now remembered on the Wall of the Missing in the fine American military cemetery and memorial at Madingley near Cambridge.

The Luftwaffe

On the eve of the Battle of Britain the Luftwaffe was really at the zenith of its power despite the losses it had incurred in the battle for France; its reputation as an all-powerful and invincible air force would never stand higher. The Luftwaffe dominated and commanded the skies from Poland to the French Atlantic coast as well as those over Denmark and Norway. And yet just four years later it could scarcely make more than a token presence over Normandy during Operation Overlord, and was steadily losing the fierce battle of attrition in the skies above the Fatherland. The rise and fall of the Luftwaffe is one of the most dramatic stories of the Second World War, and its defeat and destruction was ultimately critical to the final victory. Field Marshal Von Runsteadt later ascribed the Allies' air power and superiority as the first decisive factor in German's defeat.

One popular misconception about the German Air Force is that it owed its origins to the rise to power of Adolf Hitler. But when he became Reich Chancellor in January 1933 much of the basic foundation and

'The Wall of the Missing' at the American Cemetery and Memorial at Madingley near Cambridge.

framework of the Air Force was already in place, having been secretly developed during the 1920s. In January 1919 the Luftstreitkrate (the Army's Air Defence Arm) had been officially disbanded, and under the terms of the Versailles Armistice Agreement, which came into force in January 1920, all military aircraft manufacture was prohibited with only some 140 civil aircraft being allowed. The German Army (Reichswehr) was severely restricted to a token force of 100,000 men, but over 170 former military pilots were 'hidden' in the Army, many of whom would attain senior ranks in the wartime Luftwaffe, notably Sperrle, Kesselring and Stampff, who would each command a Luftflotte (Air Fleet).

In 1924 General von Seeckt, the head of the Reichswehr, appointed Captain Ernest Bradenburg to lead the Air Office of the Ministry of Transport, thus creating an important and critical link between civil aviation and the armed forces. The formation of the Deutscher Luftfahrtverband (DLV) – renamed Luftsport-Verband in 1933 – with strong official support and financial backing ensured that gliding became a main activity, and many famous future Luftwaffe 'aces' gained their first experience of flight with the DLV. By 1928 it had over 50,000 active members along with a large and flourishing youth movement. In 1924, as a result of the Rapallo agreement between Germany and Russia, General von Seeckt established three secret air bases in Russia, including a flying training school at Lipetsk, some 200 miles south-east of Moscow, for the training of fighter pilots on Fokker aircraft imported from Holland. The bases were also used for the trialling and development of military aircraft.

The German state civil airline, Deutsche Lufthansa, emerged in early 1926 with Erhard Milch as its operations (and later commercial) director. Within a year or so Lufthansa would be flying more passengers over longer distances than the British, French and Italian airlines put together. Its crews were able to gain valuable experience in long-distance flights, navigation and instrument flying, which impacted on the pre-war Luftwaffe. The airline also set up commercial flying schools, which could be simply converted for military use. By the 1920s German aircraft constructors, such as Ernst Heinkel, Claude Dornier, Hugo Junkers, Heinrich and George Wulf, were producing aircraft nominally civil or 'sporting' but really designed to military specifications. The successful Junkers 52 transport aircraft was just one such example and it remained in active service throughout the war.

In the early 1930s Winston Churchill had cautioned that Germany was 'In violation of the Treaty of Versailles, busy creating an air force under the guise of flying clubs, police units and commercial ventures that would soon equal and outrival the RAF.' But his timely words of warning largely went unheeded. Within a month of coming to power Adolf Hitler appointed his close colleague, Hermann Göring, an ex-First World War fighter 'ace' and commander of the famous Richtofen Geschwader (equivalent to a RAF Group), as the Reich Commissioner for Air, but it was Erhard Milch, another First World War veteran, as the new Secretary of State for Air, that undertook most of the development of the Luftwaffe. He, rather than Göring, can be considered the architect of the wartime Luftwaffe.Two of the Luftwaffe's senior wartime commanders – Albert Kesselring and Hans Jeschonneck – transferred from the Army. Kesselring commanded a Luftflotte and Jeschonneck became Chief of the General Staff.

In just three years Milch (who later became a Field Marshal) transformed the German aircraft industry, which by 1936 was

Me 109B first delivered to the Luftwaffe in the spring of 1937. (via J. Adams)

employing over 125,000 persons. New aerodromes were built with modern radio and visual navigation systems along with excellent communications. On 1st March 1935 the Reichsluftwaffe (soon shortened to the Luftwaffe) was 'officially' formed, and thereafter it was celebrated as 'German Air Force Day'. Eight days later Adolf Hitler acknowledged to the world the presence of the Luftwaffe, but it already comprised some 1,800 aircraft, to which 200 were being added each month, and 20,000 officers and men. Göring was appointed its Commander in Chief, but it was to be under the orders of Field-Marshal von Blomberg, the overall Commander of the Reich's armed forces; although in practice Göring as Reichsmarschall had virtual total control. By 1936 the Luftwaffe had grown to over 2,600 aircraft, almost equal in size to the combined British and French air forces at the time, and some 40% of Germany's defence budget was being spent on its air capabilities. Also in this year the experimental rocket research station at Peenemunde was opened. All of the Luftwaffe's aircraft of the early war years came from this period of intense development and growth.

The Spanish civil war offered the Luftwaffe an excellent testing ground for both aircraft and pilots. The formation of the fascist Condor Legion in late 1936 enabled the Luftwaffe crews to gain valuable battle experience. They were 'volunteered' for a specific tour of duty in order that the maximum number could be 'blooded'. Such famous wartime Luftwaffe pilots as Adolf Galland, Werner Mölders and Herbert Ihlefeld all served with the Legion, and the Luftwaffe developed the fighter tactics used in the Battle of Britain, as well as operating closely with the infantry and armoured vehicles, which became its hallmark during the successful 'Blitzkrieg' or 'Lightning-war' campaigns of 1939/40. The civil war also enabled the early versions of the Me 109 and Ju 87 to be trialled and tested in battle conditions. The Condor Legion flew its last missions in February 1939 so the Luftwaffe had an immediate nucleus of battle-hardened crews and pilots when it entered the Second World War. Also many of these experienced Luftwaffe officers were posted to training establishments to pass on their experience and knowledge.

Indeed in August 1939, Göring sent a message to his airmen, 'I have done my best, in the past few years, to make our Luftwaffe the largest and most powerful in the world. The creation of the Greater German Reich has been made possible by the strength and constant readiness of

Pre-war photograph of a Messerschmitt Me 110.

the Air Force. Born of the spirit of the German airmen in the first World War, inspired by faith in our Fuehrer and Commander-in-Chief – thus stands the German Air Force today, ready to carry out every command of the Fuehrer with lightning speed and undreamed-of might.'

Certainly the Luftwaffe had become 'the elite arm of the Wehrmacht' (German Armed Forces). Göring had gained special pay, allowances and conditions of service that attracted the cream of Germany's youth. His privileged political position as Hitler's right hand man ensured that the Luftwaffe was and remained an independent service, and also that it lacked for nothing in financial and manpower resources. However, the other side of the coin was that because of his importance in the Nazi heirarchy he could not be removed from control although his serious mishandling of the Luftwaffe would have merited such action. It could be said that Göring had a disastrous effect on the Luftwaffe and that he must bear some of the blame for its ultimate demise.

In May 1940 the strength of the all-conquering Luftwaffe stood at some 5,340 aircraft, of which over 1,700 were bombers and 1,730 fighters (single and twin engined). Other than in pure size alone it was a different kind of air force from that of the RAF, which was divided into four operational functions. The Luftwaffe comprised five Luftflotten, each with a strict designated area of control covering Germany and its occupied territories. Each Luftflotte was in essence a miniature air force in its own right, equipped with bombers, fighters and reconnaissance aircraft as well as its own communications system, command and administration structure. Nos 2 and 3 Luftflotten, which were almost exclusively engaged in the Battle of Britain, were commanded by Generalfeldmarschalls (equivalent to Marshal of the RAF) Kesselring and Sperrle respectively.

Of the Luftwaffe's bombers, the Dornier 17 was the oldest and perhaps least effective with a light bomb load and it would be phased out of frontline duties in late 1941. The Heinkel 111 had originally been designed as an airliner for Lufthansa, and was the backbone of the bomber force. It proved to be inadequately armed and highly vulnerable to fighter attack, although this fault was largely offset when it operated in the night bombing offensive. The fearsome Junkers 87, Stuka dive-bomber, which had hitherto terrorised and devastated ground troops, was seriously under-armed and fell easy prey to the RAF fighters, so much so that it was withdrawn from the Battle. However, it continued to operate in other theatres of war mainly when the Luftwaffe enjoyed complete air superiority. It was the Junkers 88 that was the most modern weapon in the Luftwaffe's armoury; a strong, fast and durable twin-engined bomber that was probably then the best in the world. It developed into a very versatile aircraft, also operating most successfully as a night-fighter.

The two Luftwaffe fighters – Me 109 and 110 – were formidable combat aircraft. Both were continually up-dated and refined, and served throughout the war. The former, a single engined aircraft, was produced in vast numbers – some 35,000 – but in truth by the late war years it was out-classed by the current Allied fighters. The much-vaunted Me 110 – 'Zerstorer' or 'Destroyer' – was a twin-engined, two seater and heavily-armed fighter that entered the Battle with a high reputation. However, it proved no match for the RAF fighters and really needed its own fighter escort. The aircraft found its true role later as a 'bomber destroyer' and became the mainstay of the German night-fighter force with over 6,000 being produced right up to March 1945.

Junkers 87 – the 'Stuka' dive-bombers. (via J. Adams)

Dornier 217E-4: mainly used in the 'Baedeker' bombing offensive. (via R. Hughes)

The Battle of Britain and the subsequent night-bombing offensive (which the Luftwaffe considered part of the Battle) was the first real set-back for the Luftwaffe and it was a deep blow to its prestige and reputation, from which it never fully recovered. In fact Göring's Chief of Staff would later maintain that, 'The Reichsmarschall never forgave us for not having conquered England.' The Luftwaffe now entered unknown territory and embarked on a strategic night-bombing offensive, for which it was not adequately equipped, to produce Göring's 'crippling knock-out blow'. Although its bomber crews had the advantages of the sophisticated X-Gerät radio direction beams, its main bombers, the He 111s and Ju 88s, carried an insufficient tonnage of bombs, and were not really designed for all-out strategic warfare. One of the basic flaws in the Luftwaffe's armoury was that it did not possess a heavy bomber the equal of any of the Allied heavy bomber force. Its pre-war development of long-range heavy bombers had been cancelled because of engine problems, and the Dornier 217, another twin-engined bomber which emerged in early 1941, certainly did not fit the bill although it proved to be an efficient and reliable aircraft. The Luftwaffe's only heavy bomber, Heinkel 177, 'Grief', was almost four years in development, and never fulfilled its potential – only 1,200 were produced. It should be noted that by 1942 the German aircraft industry

71

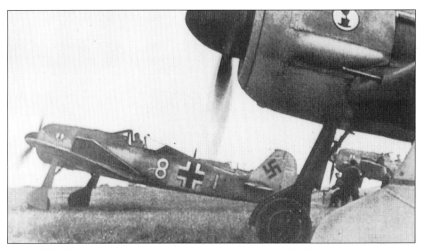

Focke-Wulf Fw 190: the aircraft that caused problems for Fighter Command.

was deeply involved in fighter production, and furthermore did not have sufficient financial investment to fund the enormous costs involved in producing a heavy bomber force.

During 1941 it could still be said that the Luftwaffe remained in a commanding and dominant position. It had sustained relatively light losses in its night-bombing campaign, and its fighters were taking a steady toll of both Bomber and Fighter Command. In the summer when Hitler launched Operation Barbarossa – the offensive against Russia – the Luftwaffe soon gained almost total air superiority over the Russian Air Force, and the invasion of Greece and the airborne assault on Crete in May showed that it was still a most formidable and powerful force. It was not until 1942 that the strain on the Luftwaffe began to tell. It was now fighting on three fronts. The Russian campaign was beginning to deplete its forces, and in the Middle East the Luftwaffe had difficulty keeping its aircraft flying in the face of mechanical problems and acute fuel shortages. On the European front the Luftwaffe had managed to keep the RAF at bay, largely on account of the introduction of their new and technically superior Focke-Wulf 190 fighter, another aircraft that would survive to the end of the war, with over 19,000 being built. However, the Luftwaffe was now facing the increasingly heavy bombing raids by Bomber Command and the growing strength of

Fighter Command's offensive wings. It was also expected to give air support to Admiral Dönitz's U-boat campaign in the North Atlantic as well as provide protection to his vital U-boat bases along the French Atlantic coast.

The Luftwaffe was still fighting the air war with essentially the same aircraft (though improved versions) that it had at the outbreak of the war. The Force was paying dearly for muddled thinking, changes of policies, and political indecisions and delays that had restricted the funding of development projects. The failure of the relatively few new aircraft that did appear meant that the existing and well tried aircraft such as the Me 109s and 110s, Fw 190s and Ju 88s were kept in production when in reality they were becoming out-dated and out-classed by the Allies' new aircraft. The Me 210, a new fighter planned as the successor to the Me 110, was something of a dismal failure, although it did bring about the Me 410 'Hornisse', which was expected to be the Luftwaffe's answer to the Mosquito, but the aircraft did not quite achieve the success hoped for it and production ceased in September 1944. Göring had greatly praised the Mosquito and famously complained, 'I wish someone had brought out a wooden aircraft for me'! The He 219 'Uhu' or 'Owl', a specialised night-fighter, fell foul of political indecision and less than 330 were produced although it was technically far superior to the old Me 110. There was now an urgent and almost desperate need to increase fighter production as the Luftwaffe faced the growing might of Bomber Command and the Eighth Air Force, so the old and tried fighters were produced in even greater numbers. In 1943 53% of the German aircraft production was devoted to fighters, and in the following year the percentage would rise to 78%! The Luftwaffe losses were now rising alarmingly; from January to October 1942 over 5,790 aircraft were lost on all war fronts, or about 90% of its strength at the beginning of the year. But despite all the efforts of the Allied strategic bombing, aircraft production increased to almost 40,000 in 1944.

1943 saw the beginning of the decline of the Luftwaffe as an effective fighting force. The Allied air assault on Germany began to take a heavy toll on industrial production, leaving towns and cities in ruins and civilian deaths increased. Over 58,000 heavy bomber sorties were made, 80% of them by Bomber Command at night, and although the German defences managed to destroy over 4,600 aircraft (4.6%), the apparent

Junkers Ju 88G-1 night-fighter, landed in error at Woodbridge in July 1944.

inability of the Luftwaffe to prevent this devastation incurred the wrath of Hitler and the opprobrium of the German people. The Luftwaffe's prestige and reputation, and that of its Commander, Göring, which had been so high just 18 months earlier, was in tatters. Furthermore it had suffered a heavy defeat in the Mediterranean, and only a token force remained on the Russian front. During the year its fighter losses averaged 25% each month, and this was before the P-51s made their entry into the European air war. On 18th August the Luftwaffe's Chief of Staff, Hans Jeschonnek, committed suicide, the day after the heavy Allied raids on Schweinfurt/Regensberg and Peenemunde. With the might of the Allied heavy bombing increasing almost daily and nightly, the Luftwaffe had no alternative other than to fight in defence of the Reich, and therein lay the seeds of its destruction.

The task facing the Luftwaffe at the beginning of 1944 was really beyond its capabilities, and it says much for the tenacity and bravery of its airmen that it survived almost to the end of the war. In the first four months of the year the day fighter force in Europe had lost over 1,000 pilots. General Adolf Galland, the famous fighter ace and now the 'Inspeckteur der Jagdflieger' (Inspector of Fighters), stated, 'the time has come when our force is within sight of collapse'; and yet during this period Galland's fighter pilots had inflicted grievous losses on both the Eighth Air Force and Bomber Command, the latter suffering its heaviest casualties on a single operation – 95 bombers lost (11.9%) over Nuremberg on 30th/31st March. Galland would be later dismissed from

Me 262: the Luftwaffe's turbo-jet fighter. (via J. Adams)

this post, just one of a number of senior Luftwaffe commanders that fell out with Göring over air policy and strategy.

From the spring, the Luftwaffe in the West began to face the full might of another 'new' Air Force – the AEAF – which was far greater in strength, tactically superior, technically better equipped, and led by more experienced commanders. According to Sperrle, the Commander of the Luftflotte 3, on 6th June 1944 he had only 300 operational aircraft, of which about a third were fighters. Indeed, in total, there were about 1,300 aircraft based in France and the Low Countries with only about half of them being serviceable! In May the Eighth Air Force began its costly but effective offensive against the German oil industry, which in the fullness of time would strangle and starve the Luftwaffe of aviation fuel. In retrospect the final twelve months of war could almost be considered as a 'no contest' between the Allied air forces and the Luftwaffe.

However, neither Hitler nor Göring saw it that way. They placed immense faith in the emergence of the Luftwaffe's new aircraft to bring about a miraculous recovery to their fortunes. And indeed there were a number of aircraft, all jet or rocket powered, that might have made some difference, had they appeared in sufficient numbers, and earlier. The first to enter operations was the Me 163 'Komet', a rocket powered fighter of advanced design. Its main drawbacks were its short operational range and its unstable and dangerous fuel; less than 400 were produced and they made little impact on the massed formations of American heavy bombers and fighters. It was the Me 262 'Schwalke' or 'Swallow', the world's first jet fighter, that offered the greatest hopes of salvation for the beleaguered Luftwaffe. It was an impressive aircraft with quite devastating fire-power, and considerable speed advantage over the Allied fighters. Since it first flew in April 1941 the aircraft's development had been dogged by technical problems and political interference, and even as late as November 1943 Hitler ordered that it be developed as a 'super-speed bomber', which further delayed its entry into the war as an interceptor. About 1,430 were produced, and had they arrived on the scene earlier and in greater numbers, it has been accepted that they might have made some difference. Also the Luftwaffe had the first jet powered bomber, the Arado Ar 234 'Blitz', which first saw action in December 1944, but by then the Luftwaffe's severe fuel shortages curtailed its operational use. However, it was an Ar 234 that made the final Luftwaffe sortie, a reconnaissance flight, over the United Kingdom on 10th April 1945.

There were other aircraft, which although technically sound and quite advanced, arrived on the scene far, far too late. The Focke-Wulf Ta 152, a high altitude fighter, the Heinkel He 162 'Volksjäger' or 'People's Fighter', a simple and cheap fighter planned to be produced in its thousands monthly, and the Bachem Ba 349 'Natter', a rocket powered vertical take-off fighter, all saw little or no action in the last few months of the war. In January 1945 the Luftwaffe still comprised over 4,500 aircraft and over 675,000 airmen but one of its critical problems was the acute shortage of trained pilots and crews. Operation 'Bodenplatte' on New Year's Day had resulted in the loss of over 220 aircraft and pilots, many of them experienced leaders, and 14 days later another 140 pilots were lost in combat with the Eighth Air Force. The Luftwaffe was now being completely overwhelmed by the sheer might and power of the combined Allied Air Forces. In March 1945 the desperation of the Luftwaffe chiefs could be seen by the formation of the 'Sonderkommando Elbe', a special volunteer suicide unit, which was planned to ram the Eighth Air Force heavy bombers. Its only known operation came on 7th April when about 120 'suicide' pilots, encouraged by the strains of martial music over the radio, 'attacked' the Eighth Air Force formations. It was thought that eight heavy bombers were lost to ramming tactics but at quite an expense to the Luftwaffe.

At the end of the war the Luftwaffe had over 1,500 aircraft but they were widely scattered and the heterogenous units were highly disorganised and virtually non-effective. The majority of the Force had been grounded either by lack of trained pilots, spare parts or empty fuel tanks. The defeat of the all-powerful Air Force was complete and total; more than 100,000 aircraft had been destroyed with over 320,00 airmen killed. Without doubt the Luftwaffe had suffered from poor and divided leadership, a number of vital strategic errors, considerable indecison and a lack of finance on development projects, as well as bitter and constant internal strife within its commands. All of these factors greatly affected its performance as a fighting force. But in the end the Luftwaffe had been comprehensively out-produced, out-engined, and technically out-classed by the Allies' aircraft and convincingly out-fought by the airmen of the Allied Air Forces.

Airfields

It has been said that during the Second World War Britain resembled a gigantic aircraft carrier moored just off the north-west coast of Europe; although one American pilot put it more succinctly when he famously remarked that the airfields were 'thicker than fleas on a dog's back'! In the early 1930s there were just 27 RAF operational stations, but over the next five years another 25 would be planned for completion before 1939, and there were a number of other airfields that did not become operational until 1940. Warmwell was one of several purely training stations that opened in the immediate pre-war years. However, by the end of the war there were well in excess of 600 Service airfields, the majority of which had been hastily constructed during 1940 to 1943, but of this large number of wartime airfields, just three – Henstridge, Hurn and Tarrant Rushton – are included in this account.

The development of airfields during the Second World War was a massive building programme conducted on a colossal scale, possibly one of the most ambitious construction projects ever undertaken in this country, especially considering the urgency and strict time restraints imposed on the contractors. At its wartime peak, in 1942, over one third of the construction industry was dedicated to the building operations, and the airfield programme received top priority in the allocation of scarce manpower resources, often to the detriment of the clearance of bombed buildings. Most of the well-known names in civil engineering – John Laing & Son Ltd, Sir Alfred McAlpine, George Wimpey & Co Ltd, W & C French Ltd, and Richard Costain Ltd – were engaged in the quite

Aerial view of Hurn, June 1942. (Bournemouth International Airport via Mike Phipp)

immense enterprise, as well as a myriad of smaller local sub-contractors. In 1942 alone, £145 million (about £3½ billion in today's values) was expended on new airfields and improvements to existing ones. All the construction work was under the control and general direction of the Air Ministry Directorate General, more endearingly known as 'Works and Bricks' or more cynically as 'Wonders and Blunders'! It was estimated that each completed wartime airfield cost in the region of £1 million.

The responsibility of selecting suitable airfield sites lay with the Air Ministry's Aerodromes Board, and it was said that by 1940 the Board had identified some 4,000 possible or likely sites in Britain, though in the event just over 10% were ultimately developed. These were in addition to the requisition of all existing private and civil aerodromes, whether they were eventually used by the Air Ministry or not. The Board's broad rule of thumb was that the site should be as close as possible to sea level or at least not above 600 feet, because of the greater risk of hill fog and low cloud; for instance Hurn is only 36 feet above mean sea level, Warmwell at 207 feet and Tarrant Rushton lies at 300 feet. The land was also required to be relatively flat and free from obstructions, both natural and man-made, and full cognizance had be taken of any existing or planned airfields in the vicinity. The guiding principle was that three miles was considered the minimum distance for operational safety, though the Board usually erred on the side of safety, and normally worked to a tolerance limit of five miles.

Once a promising and likely site had been identified by reference to extant records, such as the AA Register of Airfields, or more usually the one inch Ordnance Survey maps, it was then examined by a surveyor, on foot, field by field. Careful notes were made of any particular construction problems that might be encountered, and the nature of the sub-soil was determined; good drainage was considered to be an essential prerequisite, especially as many of the early wartime airfields were only grass surfaced. The next step in the procedure was to obtain the necessary legal planning permission under the Defence Regulations of the Emergency Powers (Defence) Act, 1939. It was at this stage that any local objections could be voiced and considered, though it must be admitted that few appeals were upheld except perhaps those raised by the Army Council. The most frequent and cogent opposition came from the War Agricultural Committee, who were equally hard-pressed to utilise all available agricultural land for the production of valuable food; the construction of each wartime airfield resulted in the loss, on average, of some 500 acres, and in most cases it was prime agricultural land.

Once the initial building contract had been awarded hordes upon hordes of building workers moved in to camp alongside the site, bringing with them large earth-moving equipment, heavy tractors and lorries, and cement mixers. Roads in the area were either closed or clogged with heavy traffic; some roads would not reopen for the rest of the war. The peace of the rural countryside was comprehensively shattered, especially as on occasions the construction work carried on day and night, such was the urgent need for airfields. For many months

79

the whole area resembled a battlefield, land was flattened, trees uprooted, ditches and hollows filled in, trenches were dug for water mains, sewerage pipes and telephone lines. In next to no time the site would either become a sea of mud or disappear under thick clouds of choking dust according to the season. Those local residents who lived through the construction period, which on average lasted about twelve months, remembered it as their single worst experience of the war! These airfields would leave an indelible mark on the local landscape; the sheer bulk of the large black hangars, the high gaunt water towers and the presence of low-flying aircraft ensured that the countryside would never be the same again.

The first real construction work was the provision of a concrete perimeter road. Normally 50 feet wide, right around the extent of the airfield, it could stretch for at least three miles or more. This road would give access to the aircraft dispersal points, more generally known as hard standings. As early as February 1939 the Air Ministry had decreed that all aircraft should be dispersed around the perimeter of the airfield as a precaution against aerial attack. The hard standings were of two types – 'frying pan' or 'spectacle or loops'. The former could be found in varying diameters up to 125 feet and the latter became standard on bomber airfields. Hurn was particularly well provided with hard standings – 30 pans and 46 loops – and Warmwell had eventually 36 pans of different sizes.

Normally the next stage was the laying of concrete, paved or asphalt runways. Most pre-war airfields had been provided with grass 'runs' and not until mid-1939 was it decided that all future bomber stations would be provided with 'firm runways'. However, Christchurch and Warmwell had grass runs, as did Henstridge, which was built during 1942/3 – even at this stage of the war fighter training stations were not normally provided with firm runways. However, Henstridge did have the distinction of being one of only two airfields in the county with five runways, grass or otherwise. Two of them were in parallel so that one could be used for practice deck landings, and it was provided with arrestor wires as found on aircraft carriers. It should be noted that there had been considerable experimental work conducted during the 1930s to find the most suitable grass seed as regard to wear and tear, and the speed of evaporation and absorption of water. One of the Air Ministry's final tests for grassed airfields was to drive a car across the completed

Laying concrete runways. (John Laing plc)

airfield at a speed of 20 mph without causing too much discomfort to the driver!

The prescribed lengths of firm runways changed during 1940/1 but ultimately a standard specification was arrived at, which became known as a Class A Standard bomber station layout. The main runway measured 2,000 yards by 50 yards wide with two subsidiaries, each 1,400 yards long, and there was normally a cleared area of 100 yards at each end as an 'overshoot'. Initially the runways were constructed of asphalt, although later concrete was universally used. They were sited to be as near as 60° to each other as possible, and were invariably in the shape of the letter 'A'. It was estimated that over 160 million square yards of concrete were laid down at these wartime airfields, which was said to be 'sufficient to complete a 9,000 mile road 30 feet wide to run from London to Peking'! This wartime concrete appears to have survived the rigours of time considering the speed in which it was laid, with several strips of perimeter roads, hard standings and runways still to be seen at the edges of fields, often the sole links to a wartime past.

There were, however, several types of 'temporary' metal track runways used during the Second World War to great effect, such as Sommerfeld Track, Pierced Steel Plank (PSP) and Square Mesh Track (SMT). These tracks were used both in this country and on the Continent after D-Day mainly for Advanced Landing Grounds, although they were also provided for more permanent fighter airfields, especially those used by the USAAF's heavy (7 tons) P-47s or Thunderbolts. Thus during the winter of 1943/4 a single SMT runway of 1,600 yards by 150 yards wide was put down at Christchurch, which involved piping the River Mude under the tracked runway in order to produce the required length. SMT, produced by British Reinforced Engineering Co, consisted of 3" square lightweight steel welded mesh backed by hessian, and was similar to that used in road building. The track was supplied in rolls 7' 3" wide and 77' 3" long and was quick and easy to lay. Although men of No 5005 Airfield Construction squadron undertook the initial construction work, it was the American 833rd Engineer Battalion (Aviation) that laid the tracking, which was ready for use towards the end of January 1944.

The most distinctive and prominent landmarks on any airfield were the large black hangars. The word comes from the French to describe 'a covered space for a carriage'! In the First World War and for many years afterwards they were known more simply as 'aircraft sheds'. There were three types of hangars to be seen on the Dorset airfields – Bellman, Type T2s and Blister. The first dated from 1937 and was named after its designer, N. S. Bellman, an engineer with the Air Ministry. Made of steel it was developed by Head & Wrightson Co Ltd, and became the Service's first transportable hangar, being quick and relatively simple to erect. The Bellman had a span of almost 88 feet, was 175 feet long and usually had about 26 feet height clearance. By 1940 over 400 Bellmans had been provided but they did become rather outdated with the appearance of larger operational aircraft, although some remained at both Hurn and Warmwell.

Engineers of 833rd Engineer Battalion (Aviation) laying Square Mesh Track at Christchurch, October 1943. (Smithsonian Institution)

It was the Type T hangars ('T' stood for Transportable) that were more prevalent at wartime airfields, of which T2s were provided for Class A Standard airfields. The hangars had been developed and built by Tees-Side Bridge & Engineering Works and were of galvanised corrugated iron construction, again they were specially designed to be simple and speedy to erect. The Type T hangars came in various sizes but T2s were 240 feet long with an opening span of 113½ feet and a door height of 25 feet – quite formidable structures, many of which have survived to this day. Most wartime airfields were provided with two T2 hangars usually sited at opposite sides of the airfield, as was the case with Warmwell. However, both Tarrant Rushton and Hurn, because of their involvement with support squadrons of the airborne forces, each had four such hangars; it was felt that the wooden gliders needed protection from the ravages of British winters.

Henstridge, Hurn and Warmwell were all provided with a number of Blister hangars. These were of a far simpler construction, and comprised arched wooden or welded steel ribs covered by curved sheets of corrugated iron sheeting, and came in two lengths – either 25 or 45 feet. They were cheap and simple to produce, and because they did not require any foundations or floorings, they were flexible enough to be erected on uneven ground. They were first produced by C. Miskins & Sons Ltd for the Service in 1939 and over 3,000 were supplied to the RAF, mainly at fighter and flying training stations.

One of the most recognisable features of any wartime airfield was the watch-house or watch-office, which later became universally known as the control tower, as they were first known in America. This building was the airfield's nerve centre of the air traffic control and was fully equipped with telephone lines, radio and tele-printer apparatus and later radar. By 1942 a fairly standard design had been developed, which was a very functional and almost square two-storied building, approximately 35 feet by 34 feet, constructed of brick and rendered with cement. The tower had a railed balcony as well as railings on the flat roof, and some buildings were provided with an external iron stairway. There are many poignant wartime images of the balcony crowded with senior officers waiting in apprehension for the first sound and sight of the returning aircraft. The Admiralty developed its own particular type of control tower; they were larger than the RAF towers, three storeys instead of two and usually supplied with a glasshouse on the flat roof –

A wartime control tower, which was built to a standard design.

a design feature taken up by the RAF in the immediate post-war years. Henstridge's control tower is a good example of RNAS towers, having survived by being converted into a residential house; as has the control tower at Warmwell. Although modified and improved over the years the control tower at Bournemouth International Airport still betrays its early wartime construction.

Close to the control tower and inscribed in large white letters was the airfield's unique identification code – two letters about 10 feet in size. These date back to pre-war days when it became the practice to display the name of the aerodrome in white letters sufficiently large to be visible from an altitude of about 2,000 feet. For obvious security reasons this method was suspended during the war and the letter code was substituted; Christchurch's code was 'XC', Hurn 'KU', Tarrant Rushton 'TK', and Warmwell 'XW', and all were for day use only. The letters became more commonly known as the 'Pundit Code' from the mobile beacon unit (known as a 'pundit'), which flashed the airfield's code in red morse signals at night.

There was a multiplicity of administrative, operational and technical buildings around the airfield, from the armoury to the water tower.

There were headquarters sections, workshops, an operations block, photographic section, sick quarters, vehicle repair areas, equipment and parachute stores, briefing rooms, dispersal huts, a guard-house, a cinema, NAAFI, kitchens, messes, a gymnasium and so on. Most of these buildings were prefabricated huts, some of timber and plasterboard, while others were of pre-cast concrete, and the Orlit, Maycrete and Laing huts seemed to be the most prevalent. The living quarters necessary to accommodate maybe in excess of 2,500 officers and men were generally rather spartan, and were mainly provided by the curved corrugated sheet-iron Nissen huts, which owed their origins to the First World War and a certain Canadian Colonel P. Nissen. These huts of varying spans – from 16, 24 and 30 feet – probably epitomise wartime airfields more than any other structure. They are often fondly remembered by wartime airmen despite their reputation for being bitterly cold in winter and oppressively hot in the summer, and the term 'running water' normally meant leaking roofs and heavy condensation – but perhaps the distance of time has lent enchantment to the memory? However, Nissen huts were still being used by the British forces in the Falklands conflict. Some of the old wartime buildings have survived the test of time. Warmwell's one-time NAAFI, cinema and gymnasium is now used as a village hall, and a number of wartime buildings can still be identified at Hurn.

As the construction of the airfield came near to conclusion, the question of a system of defence was determined, the contractor liaising

Tarrant Rushton's control tower being demolished in 1981. (Flight Refuelling Ltd via Colin Cruddas)

A wartime T2 hangar still in use at Tarrant Rushton.

closely with the local military commander as to the siting of pillboxes and other defences. Most airfields were provided with pillboxes around the perimeter normally not less than half a mile apart, with a second ring of pillboxes dispersed to cover the external approaches to the airfields. In 1940, before the formation of the RAF Regiment, the responsibility of the airfield's defence lay with the Station Commander. In June of that year Winston Churchill had stated that 'each airman should have his place in the defence scheme. It must be understood by all ranks that they are expected to fight and die in the defence of their airfields.' By the autumn a new RAF trade of 'ground gunner' had been formed, and before the year was out almost 40,000 were engaged in airfield defence. For instance at Christchurch, in late 1940, some 140 airmen together with over two dozen Army personnel were engaged in defence, armed with four Bofors guns, two dozen Lewis guns and a 1.5 pounder gun, as well as an armoured car known as an Armadillo and a quantity of ordinary .303 rifles.

The vast majority of wartime airfields in the country have long since disappeared; many have returned to farming while others have vanished under industrial and residential development. In Dorset only Hurn and Henstridge are still used for their original purpose, but at the extreme ends of a very wide spectrum – an International Airport compared with a small private flying field. Christchurch and Warmwell have succumbed to housing and industrial estates, with the latter's airfield being used for gravel extraction. Tarrant Rushton survived as a working airfield until 1980 but has now returned to agricultural use. Even as early as November 1943 when the last wartime airfields were becoming operational, the Air Ministry had recognised there would be a sudden and rapid demise in the immediate post-war years, and the vast resources devoted to their construction would not represent 'an asset of abiding value' but rather be 'a very considerable liability for the reinstatement of sites and the restoration of land to its former uses' – remarkable prescience!

2

CHRISTCHURCH

From being a small and relatively minor pre-war aerodrome, Christchurch developed into an important wartime airfield. This was mainly due to the presence of the aircraft production factory of Airspeed (1934) Ltd, which produced a number of its very famous training aircraft, the Oxford, there, as well as its equally impressive and successful glider, the Horsa. For a brief period during the summer of 1944 Christchurch became a fully operational station when under the control of the USAAF, the airfield and surrounding town and countryside reverberated to the raucous sounds of the Pratt and Whitney engines of the rugged P-47s that were engaged on missions across the Channel before and after D-Day.

However, before Airspeed (1934) Ltd set up residence the airfield played host to a wide variety of aircraft from Avro Ansons to Armstrong Whitworth Whitleys; the diversity of aircraft using the grassed strips during 1940/1 could scarcely be equalled by any other RAF airfield. They were all playing a part in what has been described as that 'Most Secret War' – the development of Radio Direction Finding (RDF), both airborne and ground, which later would become better known as Radar – an American acronym for 'radio detecting and ranging'. Basically RDF was the fixing of an aircraft's position by the use of radio signals converging on it from a number of ground stations.

Like all private airfields throughout the country Christchurch was requisitioned by the Air Ministry at the outbreak of the war. Only a couple of months earlier it had been considered a likely site for an aerial bombing range, but the Air Ministry did not pursue the proposal as other plans were afoot for Christchurch. The Air Defence Experimental Establishment, which had been based at Biggin Hill for a number of years, had already moved into the area. The ADEE was engaged in highly secret work on RDF airborne interception; indeed, as early as 1936 Gloster Gauntlets of No 32 squadron had carried out the first successful RDF controlled interception during an Empire Air Day display at Biggin Hill, although the thousands of spectators present were quite unaware that they had witnessed a historic and important event. The ADEE would be joined by the Searchlight Experimental Establishment and the Army RDF team, both engaged on ground radar defence projects, and the Units would become known as the Air Defence Research and Development Establishment (ADRDE).

Early in May 1940 another highly secret unit, the Air Ministry Research Establishment, moved into the county – at Worth Matravers near Swanage. It had originally been established at Bawdsey Manor in Suffolk in February 1936, where Robert A. Watson-Watt and his team devised the chain of RDF defences that proved to be so critical to the outcome of the Battle of Britain. The move of this secret unit, soon to be known as the Telecommunications Research Establishment (TRE), from its temporary home in Dundee, directly involved RAF Christchurch. On 8th May the Special Duty Flight arrived from St Athan near Cardiff under the command of Squadron Leader P. E. Meagher. This Flight would undertake the necessary airborne trials for both research units.

For this task the Flight was equipped initially with Fairey Battles, Bristol Blenheims, Avro Ansons and Handley Page Harrows, which were later augmented with a Supermarine Walrus, Vickers Wellington, Douglas Boston, de Havilland Fox Moth, Gloster Gladiator, and even a Bristol Beaufighter, then a very new and scarce aircraft. Three Hawker Hurricanes were provided to afford protection for the Flight's aircraft as well as the airfield; one of these, L1592, miraculously survived the war to become part of the National Aeronautical Collection and is housed in the Flight Gallery of the Science Museum in London bearing the codes 'KW-Z' of No 615 squadron. It had been the 46th Hurricane to come off the production line at Kingston-on-Thames, Surrey in early 1938 and in June of that year the aircraft was allocated to No 56, but would later serve in Nos 17, 43 and 615 squadrons, the latter two during the Battle of

Hawker Hurricane, L1592, on display in the Science Museum. (Science & Society Picture Library)

Britain. The Hurricane was twice badly damaged during the Battle, and it had also been flown by a well-known Battle of Britain pilot, Pilot Officer Anthony Woods-Scawen, who was unfortunately killed in action in September 1940. L1592 was transferred to the Special Duty Flight in October 1940 and it remained at Christchurch until the following August. For the remainder of the war the aircraft served in a variety of maintenance and training units, and then, in 1952, appeared in the film *Angels One-Five*, but was only shown on the ground. Two years later the aircraft was acquired by the Science Museum, and in 1961 it was rebuilt by Hawkers. The Hurricane went on display in the new Aviation Gallery when the Gallery first opened in July 1963, and is the sole surviving Battle of Britain Hurricane.

An aircraft that was very familiar to the local residents at Christchurch, the Avro 504, appeared the following month – shades of pre-war days when Captain Fisher had offered pleasure flights at the airfield! Just three of these famous and quite remarkable aircraft arrived for a brief stay. They were to act as tugs for the Scott Viking sailplanes (the pre-war name for gliders) that would test whether the RDF equipment at Worth Matravers could actually detect the approach of wooden gliders. Once the highly secret tests had been completed successfully, the Avro 504s left Christchurch for a final time.

With the fall of France there was a concern about the vulnerability of the airfield to Luftwaffe attacks. This was especially so as the aircraft factory was now taking shape alongside the western edge of the airfield, and actually located on the original site of the first Somerford (Christchurch) landing ground. In August 1940 it was decided to disperse some of the Flight's aircraft to a small grassed emergency landing ground at Sway, about six miles to the north-east of Christchurch, which was thought to be less likely to attract the Luftwaffe's attention. However, the dispersal was not very practical because of the nature of the Flight's experimental work and the idea was soon abandoned. Strangely, the airfield at Sway was bombed by the Luftwaffe in early April 1941.

In June, Flight Lieutenant H. E. Bufton and Corporal Mackie, his radio operator, of the Wireless Intelligence Development Unit then stationed at Boscombe Down in Wiltshire, left in one of the Flight's Ansons for RAF Wyton in Cambridgeshire. The intention was to fly up the east coast in an attempt to locate and track the origin and course of a German radio direction signal; intelligence sources had revealed the possible existence of a fairly primitive system, which the Luftwaffe was using as a navigational aid. The flight was successful, the beams did in fact exist and were transmitted from ground stations at Bredstedt and Kleve. The system, code-named 'Knickebein' (translated as 'Crooked or Dog Leg'), was successfully jammed but the more complicated system 'X-Gerät' was used very effectively by the Luftwaffe when Coventry was heavily bombed in November. The Flight's Ansons were subsequently transferred to the WIDU, which in December 1940 became No 109 Special Duties (wireless) squadron. Hal Bufton was one of three brothers that served with distinction in the RAF; his elder brother Sydney, a Group Captain in the Air Ministry, was one of the earliest proponents of a 'target-finding' or Pathfinder Force. The third brother, John, was killed whilst flying Hampdens with No 83 squadron.

During September 1940 the Special Duty Flight accounted for three enemy aircraft. On the 2nd of the month Squadron Leader Meagher in a Hurricane shot down a Junkers 88 about ten miles south-west of the Needles. Flight Lieutenant Douglas L. Rayment destroyed a Junkers 88 on the 12th whilst he was engaged in an experimental flight in a Blenheim, then a week later he was flying a   Hurricane when he accounted for another Junkers 88. It is a trifle unfortunate that neither of these pilots would be awarded the coveted Battle of Britain Clasp, because only those flying operational sorties with certain listed squadrons were eligible for the award. Rayment was, however, awarded the AFC in July 1941, but his Blenheim failed to return on the 17th of the month, and he and his wireless operator/gunner, Sergeant R. Sadler, were posted as missing.

In October 1940 Wing Commander G. K. Horner assumed command of the Flight, and in the following month 'H' Flight of No 2 Anti-aircraft Co-operation Unit moved in from Gosport, from where it had been operating since before the war. Gosport was one of a number of airfields that had sustained heavy damage during August, when three raids from Junkers 87s had put the airfield out of action and it would be early December before it could be used again operationally. The Flight's mixed bag of aircraft – Fairey Battles, Blenheims, Miles Magisters and Westland Lysanders – flew trial and experimental sorties for the scientists of the ADRDE until it was disbanded at the end of June 1941.

By the New Year the Government's 'shadow factory', as they were known, had been completed. This strange name, which perhaps hints at rather sinister connotations, dated from 1934 with the expansion of munitions production in the country, and when new Government sponsored factories were constructed under what was then known as the 'shadow scheme'. Its connection with the aircraft industry came two years later in the wake of the rapid expansion of the RAF, when it was decided to utilise the expertise of motor manufacturers in mass production to increase the country's output of aircraft. Most of the early shadow factories were thus linked to motor manufacturers, such as Rootes at Speke, Standard Motors at Coventry, Morris Motors at Cowley and Austin at Longbridge, and they were invariably sited in the Midlands.

However, by 1938 the Air Ministry was under considerable pressure to increase aircraft production even more; under the latest RAF Expansion Scheme 'L' it was planned to produce 12,000 new military aircraft in three years. A decision was taken to apply the shadow scheme to existing aircraft manufacturers. The Government would provide the new shadow factories, which would be managed by aircraft companies for an agreed agency fee. These new factories would require airfields or at least basic landing ground facilities for flight testing and delivery, although it must be admitted that such combined sites were rare, so Christchurch proved to be quite a bonus for the Ministry of Aircraft Production, even though it was situated in a somewhat vulnerable position, more especially after the fall of France. Certainly without the existence of these shadow factories it would have been quite impossible for the country's aircraft production to have achieved parity with Germany by the outbreak of war, let alone to exceed it by 1940.

The factory at Christchurch would be managed by Airspeed (1934) Ltd, which had its main factory at Portsmouth, where it had moved from York in March 1933. The company had originally been co-founded by N. S. Norway, more famous as the novelist Nevil Shute, and one of its original directors (of the 1934 company) was Sir Alan Cobham. In 1940 de Havilland Aircraft Co. had acquired a controlling interest in

A fine flight of Airspeed Oxfords – pupil pilots practising formation flying.

Airspeed, and was already building the company's best known and most successful RAF aircraft, the AS.10 Oxford, under contract at its factory at Hatfield in Hertfordshire.

The Oxford, or 'Ox-box' as it was more commonly known to RAF airmen, was the result of an Air Ministry specification, T23/36, for a twin-engined trainer. Airspeed specifically developed the Oxford from its moderately successful small passenger airliner the AS.6 Envoy, which had first flown in June 1934; the Oxford's ultimate overwhelming success revived the somewhat ailing fortunes of the company.

The Oxford made its first public appearance in the 'New Type Park' at Hendon during the annual RAF Display of June 1937, and it entered the Service five months later with the Central Flying School, to become the first twin-engined monoplane for advanced flying training. For its time the Oxford was a rather remarkable aircraft with dual controls as standard. Normally manned by three crew, it provided six crew stations for various training duties, and besides purely pilot training it had facilities for pupil navigators, bomb aimers, air gunners and radio and camera operators. Without doubt it was the most complete training aircraft yet produced for the RAF. Moreover the small but sturdy aircraft had handling qualities specifically designed to match those of far larger and heavier aircraft. It was said that 'if you could handle the Oxford [not an easy aeroplane to fly] with reasonable competence, you could tackle almost anything in the way of recalcitrant twins and multis.' The Oxford I was provided with an Armstrong Whitworth dorsal turret, whereas in the Mark II it had been removed. Both Marks were powered by two Armstrong Siddeley Cheetah radial engines, and flat out they could be nursed to over 185 mph but cruised at a more leisurely pace of about 140 mph. Although their main role was aircrew advanced training, they also operated as air ambulances (adapted under Specification 8/40), and for general communication duties, along with radar calibration work, beam approach training and as target-tugs. Oxfords operated in flying training schools in Canada, Australia, New Zealand, Southern Rhodesia and the Middle East. In total 8,586 Oxfords, in four Marks, were produced, almost 5,000 by the parent company at Portsmouth or Christchurch, the last production aircraft leaving the Portsmouth factory on 14th July 1945. At the end of the war the RAF had over 4,100 on complement, the second most numerous aircraft to the Spitfire. Oxfords remained in service with the RAF at training schools until 1954 – 17 years of sterling service.

On 30th April 1941 quite literally 'out of the blue' a German biplane, resplendent in its Luftwaffe markings – the black Iron Crosses – landed at the airfield. It was a Bücker Bü 131 Jungmann, which was a classic two-seat training aircraft. Two former French Air Force pilots, Denys Boudard and Jean Hebert, had managed to steal the aircraft from Caen airfield, and successfully fly it across the Channel undetected by either the German or British RDF systems. Both pilots ultimately served in the RAF but Hebert was lost in action during 1943.

Almost as if in retaliation for this audacious flight the Luftwaffe made two rather inconsequential attacks on the airfield during May. The first came on the 10th of the month and was made by a solitary Heinkel 111, the bombs causing only minimal damage to some huts and nearby residential property. Two days later a second raid was equally unsuccessful. Steps were now taken to camouflage the airfield and aircraft factory with quite obvious effectiveness because the Luftwaffe never returned. Although as Leslie Dawson illustrates in his excellent book *Wings Over Dorset*, this may be due to a German reconnaissance photograph, which incorrectly identified the Airspeed factory and the research establishment as a 'Flugzeugzellenreparaturwerk' or 'Aircraft repair works'!

The Ministry of Aircraft Production always had a strong proprietorial interest in what the Ministry considered *their* airfields (although few actually were!). The RAF units that happened to share the facilities at such airfields were made to feel that they were there under sufferance; nothing but nothing, the Ministry felt, should interfere with the all-important and over-riding task of producing aircraft. Indeed, the history of the British aircraft industry from 1936 to 1945 was a truly outstanding success story, with over 120,000 aircraft built in the war years, almost a quarter of them being training and communication aircraft. By March 1944 the industry employed over 1.7 million people, of which the majority were women; in that year alone 26,500 aircraft were built, an increase of nearly 800% on the pre-war figures! As the production of Oxfords began at Christchurch (550 were ultimately built there), the days of the Special Duty Flight at Christchurch were severely numbered. A new airfield under construction at nearby Hurn would become its new home, and the Flight finally severed its links with Christchurch in early November. 'H' Flight of the Anti-aircraft Co-operation Unit was disbanded at the end of June, but the airfield did not quite become the sole preserve of Airspeed (1934) Ltd, as the Fleet Air Arm moved into the Flight's old accommodation to set up an experimental station for fitting radar equipment into Naval aircraft; HMS *Raven*, as it became known, would remain at Christchurch until 1946.

Airspeed's design team had moved from Portsmouth to de Havilland's factory at Hatfield in the summer of 1940 largely, I suspect, on account of the heavy Luftwaffe raids on Portsmouth. It was at Hatfield that they began working on a new aircraft under Air Ministry specification, T24/40, for a single-seater trainer, which was provisionally numbered AS.49. Unfortunately Hatfield airfield was bombed on 3rd October 1940 and the mock-up of the new aircraft along with all the drawings and calculations were destroyed; the project was not resuscitated. The team, led by A. E. Ellison, moved into Salisbury House near London Colney, and it proved to be a most propitious move because here they worked alongside the de Havilland design team engaged in developing the famous 'wooden wonder' – the Mosquito. This fine old manor house would now also see the creation of another successful wooden 'aircraft' – the AS.51 Horsa glider.

The Air Ministry specification, X22/40, authorised Airspeed to produce the first 20 troop-carrying gliders, and it was quickly followed by X23/40 for the Horsa's subsequent development and production. In many ways the Horsa might be considered Airspeed's greatest achievement. The glider was of a high wing and all wood construction – laminated spruce and plywood beneath a cover of doped fabric – and even the cockpit controls were fashioned from wood. It was designed to be built in 30 separate sections, which would be assembled and test-flown from RAF Maintenance Units. There were two Marks produced, Mark I to carry 25 fully-equipped troops, and the Mark II (AS.58) with a hinged nose for the direct loading of a vehicle, such as the new American light truck known as a 'jeep', along with light guns; it was also provided with twin nosewheels. The Horsa had a wing span of 88 feet and was 67 feet in length (the Mark II was almost a foot longer), with a maximum towing speed of 150 mph although its normal gliding speed was in the region of about 100 mph.

The first Horsa I (DG 597) made its maiden flight on 12th September 1941 from Fairey Aviation's Great West Aerodrome (now part of London Heathrow) with G. B. S. Ellington, the company's chief test pilot, at the controls, and the glider was towed by an Armstrong Whitworth

Airspeed AS.51 Horsa gliders. (RAF Museum)

Whitley. It was a significant event because never before had such a large glider been towed, although six months later it would be almost dwarfed by another new glider – the General Aircraft G.A.L.49 Hamilcar. The Horsas would make their first entry into operations with Operation Husky – the invasion of Sicily in July 1943 – when 27 of the 30 Horsas that had survived the long tow-flight from the United Kingdom to North Africa went into action. The gliders went on to play significant parts in the four major airborne operations of the war – D-Day, the landings in southern France, Arnhem and the crossing of the Rhine in March 1945, carrying both British and American airborne troops.

By the summer of 1942 glider manufacture was afforded a high priority on the direct instruction of the War Cabinet. The initial order for Horsas had been doubled, then later trebled and more urgent demands would follow in due course, as the Airborne Force was rapidly increased. It would appear from de Havilland's figures that 3,655 Horsas were produced in total; some 2,900 were sub-contracted to furniture manufacturers, notably Harris Lebus and Elliott's of Newbury, although Austin Motor Co built some 360. The Airspeed factory at

Airspeed (1934) Ltd modified Spitfire Vs into Seafires.

Christchurch produced 695 and it was the only place where the gliders were built, assembled and test-flown from a single site. Later Airspeed produced a bomb-carrying glider, AS.52, and also a powered version, but neither saw operational service. The Horsa was the main British assault glider of the Second World War, and Brigadier-General G.J.S. Chatterton, who commanded the Glider Pilot Regiment, would later comment, 'the Horsa gave great service to the Airborne Forces and its building was one of the supreme efforts of the Second World War.'

In addition to the steady production of Oxfords and Horsas at Christchurch, in 1943 the company was awarded a sub-contract to convert Spitfires into Seafires for the Fleet Air Arm as the Naval version of the famous fighter. After the successful operations of Sea Hurricanes from aircraft carriers, it was decided to trial Spitfires in this role. The first carrier landings of Spitfire Vs took place in late 1941 and when the trials had been successfully accomplished, the green light was given to convert Mark Vs into Seafires with the provision of arrestor hooks beneath the fuselages as well as catapult spools. Some 160 Seafire conversions would be undertaken at Christchurch.

The relatively small grassed landing area at Christchurch was hardly

P-47 (Thunderbolt) resplendent in D-Day markings. (Smithsonian Institution)

adequate for the aircraft now using the airfield, and there were a number of unfortunate landing accidents. Although the Whitleys that were used to tow the assembled Horsas appeared to be large and ponderous aircraft, this was deceptive as they could actually operate safely from quite small airfields. However, as has already been noted, the airfield began to have a face-lift in October 1943, as the Air Ministry had allocated the airfield to the USAAF for use as a forward operational fighter base. Early in the New Year the Taylorcraft Austers of No 652 (AOP) squadron arrived for a brief stay. This aircraft was exceedingly light in construction, indeed it was the manufacturer's proud boast that the tail section could be easily lifted by 'a young lady'! They were also blessed with the ability to require a very short take-off and landing run, and although they appeared fragile, the aircraft proved to be quite rugged, becoming indispensable for Army support duties, especially with the 2nd TAF on the Continent. The Austers had left Christchurch before the American airmen descended upon the airfield in great numbers.

It was at the end of February 1944 that the advance party of the 405th

Fighter/Bomber Group of Ninth Air Force arrived at Christchurch, followed by the main contingent on 6th March; Christchurch now became known as Station 416. The Group had been placed in the 84th Fighter Wing, along with other Fighter Groups operating from Winkton, Beaulieu and Lymington. Each USAAF Fighter Group comprised three squadrons normally commanded by a Major (equivalent to a Squadron Leader); Nos 509 to 511 made up the 405th Group, each with their own squadron codes – G9, 2Z and K4 respectively – which were painted on the aircraft's fuselage to the left of the American white star. They also had coloured nosebands and bands across the fins and tails. The Group was equipped with about 75 Republic P-47s (Thunderbolts).

This aircraft was probably the most famous American fighter of the Second World War, being built in larger numbers than any other. It was variously described as the 'Jug' (Juggernaut), the 'Flying Milk Bottle' or 'The Repulsive Scatterbolt' because it was so unlike the conventional idea of a sleek, compact and streamlined fighter. The first prototype had flown in May 1941 and it was in service with the USAAF by September 1942. The P-47 was noticeably different from its contemporary fighters, almost twice the weight of a Spitfire and even heavier than a Blenheim. It was a very rugged aircraft, capable of sustaining quite heavy damage but still surviving. Despite its bulk the aircraft was fast, especially at high altitudes, with a quite frightening rate of dive, and was one of the heaviest armed fighters of the time, with eight .50 machine guns. In spite of a few bad habits, the P-47 engendered a terrific loyalty from its pilots. Although much of its thunder was stolen by the P-51 Mustangs, the two top fighter 'aces' of the USAAF flew P-47s throughout the war, a sufficient testimony to the aircraft's capability and success as a combat fighter. As the Group's designation suggested, the P-47 was also a most effective strike fighter/bomber in the style of the RAF's Typhoon, capable of carrying two 1,000 pound bombs.

The Group's Commanding Officer, Colonel James Ferguson, was not particularly impressed with the accommodation for his men at Christchurch. Most were forced to live in tents in the grounds of Somerford Lodge, while the Group had set up its headquarters in the nearby Bure Homage manor house. It was not until 11th April that the pilots were considered ready for their first operation, when 54 P-47s left for a fighter sweep over north-west France. Just 15 days later the Group had a new Commander, Colonel Robert L. Delashaw, who would remain in charge throughout its short stay at Christchurch. Another 14 missions were mounted during April, including four dive-bombing operations.

In May the Group was re-designated a Fighter Group and its pilots had their first experience of escort duties for B-24s of the Eighth Air Force engaged on a bombing mission to Hanover. There would be a number of unfortunate P-47 accidents at the airfield. The first occurred on the 20th when Lieutenant John Willingham's aircraft crashed onto an empty bungalow to the south-west of the airfield. He managed to escape serious injuries; the two 500 pound bombs carried by the aircraft mercifully did not explode! It was a vastly different matter on 29th June when a P-47 piloted by 2nd Lieutenant Vincent James failed to gain height on take-off and crashed onto two bungalows in Mudeford. One of the bombs exploded, killing the airman and three civilians. Another P-47 following close behind was caught in the impact of the blast and crashed onto waste land, but Captain William Champion fortunately survived. However, whilst rescue crews were attending the first crash, the second bomb exploded, which resulted in ten further deaths and over 20 injuries. This tragic incident was the worst accident for the Ninth Air Force during its time in the United Kingdom.

On D-Day the Group was given the task of patrolling the Channel accompanied by RAF Liberators searching for enemy U-boats. Their various sweeps, bombing and strike operations after D-Day brought about a loss of pilots usually from ground flak; in total 21 P-47s went missing whilst the Group operated from Christchurch. One rather fortunate pilot, Lieutenant Dumar, baled out over the Channel on 22nd June, but was rescued by a RAF Walrus; however, the Walrus was unable to take off from the sea, so its pilot calmly taxied his aircraft back to the mainland! It was on this day that the Group's pilots first began to use No A8 Emergency Landing strip at Picauville on the Cotentin peninsula. From now on they would alternate between Picauville and Christchurch, until the Group mounted its final mission from Christchurch on 11th July. The main party moved to the Continent on that day, but the last American airmen would not leave Christchurch until a week later. Colonel Delashaw presented a Stars and Stripes flag to the Priory Church, 'to be hung in perpetuity as a symbol of unity for which both nations are now fighting.' There was a re-dedication service at the Priory in May 1985. The 405th would claim four enemy aircraft on

Lt William H. Downey, 509th Fighter Squadron, May 1944. Airspeed's buildings are in the background. (Smithsonian Institution)

4th May 1945, the last day of wartime operations; but it also had the misfortune to lose the last Ninth aircraft of the war – a P-47 crashed into a lake after 'buzzing' a POW camp.

With the departure of the Americans and their P-47s the airfield returned to relative peace and quiet. On 19th March 1945 it was transferred from No 11 Group of Fighter Command to No 46 Group of Transport Command, to act as a satellite for RAF Ibsley. In the following January the airfield was formally taken over by the Ministry of Aircraft Production and RAF Christchurch closed down. However, no account of Christchurch airfield would be complete without a brief mention of the AS.57 Ambassador airliner, which made its initial flight from Christchurch on 10th July 1947 with George Errington at the controls.

This most handsome and elegant airliner of the 1950s had come about as a result of the Brabazon Committee (1943), which, in January 1944, had laid down certain guidelines and specifications for the country's post-war requirements for commercial air transport. The Ambassador was planned to be suitable for the short-range European and other medium-range services with a capacity of about 30 passengers as a replacement for the Douglas DC-3 airliner; it ultimately carried 47 passengers and a crew of three. Work on the project began in 1943 by Arthur Hagg and his team directly from an Air Ministry specification,

The handsome and elegant AS.57 Ambassador airliner. (Flight Refuelling Ltd via Colin Cruddas)

C25/43; in the following year the design team had moved into Christchurch. The name 'Ambassador' was chosen as the obvious natural progression from its earlier Courier and Envoy aircraft. Twenty were ordered by the Ministry of Aircraft Production in September 1949, and the first British European Airways scheduled flight by an Ambassador was made to Paris on 13th March 1952, although BEA had already renamed their aircraft the *Elizabethan* in honour of the new Queen. There were 20 aircraft in BEA's Elizabethan fleet all bearing names that recalled the first Elizabethan age such as *Sir Francis Drake* and *Lord Howard of Effingham*. The last scheduled BEA Elizabethan flight was made in July 1958, although a number of Ambassadors continued to operate with other companies for many years. It was the last British passenger aircraft to be powered by piston engines.

The aircraft factory at Christchurch continued with military contracts for the development of the Vampire trainer, Sea Venom and Sea Vixen fighters until 1962 when aircraft production at Christchurch ceased, and the factory was formally closed two years later. It is now an industrial estate, but the airfield itself has long since disappeared under residential housing with many of the roads recalling its earlier heydays – Airspeed Road, Ambassador Close, the Runway etc. In December 1984 a Sea Vixen, XJ580, arrived on the site from Hurn. It had been purchased by the Sea Vixen Society, and now stands as a memorial to the airfield's more immediate past and as a fitting tribute to the aviation history of Christchurch.

3

HAMWORTHY

The title of this chapter is somewhat a misnomer. Perhaps it should have been headed 'Poole' because the account is really devoted to Poole's splendid natural harbour and its use by a variety of civil and military flying boats and seaplanes. This vast tract of water has been witness to more than its fair share of drama and excitement, and over the centuries it has sustained a multitude of activities, be they legitimate or nefarious; from shipping, fishing, shipbuilding and yachting to freebootery, piracy and smuggling. And yet in those relatively brief wartime years the harbour was equally, if not more so, alive with action. From the large and majestic flying boats of BOAC and the RAF to the smaller training seaplanes of the Fleet Air Arm – the harbour was a veritable concourse of water-borne aircraft unsurpassed anywhere in the country. For a brief period in the summer of 1944 these aircraft were forced to give way to the myriad of landing craft and rescue cutters assembling for action on the big day.

It was back in 1938 that Imperial Airways had ear-marked Poole Harbour as the likely terminal for its flying boat operations in the advent of war, when it was thought that its base at Hythe on Southampton Water (first opened in March 1937) would prove to be too vulnerable to enemy air attack. At the beginning of the war the Secretary of State for Air assumed control of both Imperial Airways and British Airways, which were the two constituent companies that would form British Overseas Airways Corporation when the enabling Act came into operation on 1st April 1940; although since November 1939 the two companies had already been operating under unified control. During the war BOAC was entirely placed at the disposal of the Government, its routes were prescribed for it, not by commercial consideration but purely for war needs. It also carried almost exclusively Government passengers and freight, as well as transporting RAF personnel and supplies to various far distant war stations.

The Corporation's headquarters was established at Airways House in Poole High Street and Poole Pottery's showrooms became its reception centre for passengers and Customs clearance. Originally BOAC's flying operations were controlled from a vessel anchored off Brownsea Island but quickly the premises of Poole Harbour Yacht Club in Salterns Way were requisitioned for the Marine Terminal, and Salterns Pier was used for the high-speed launches of the Corporation and the Ministry of Aviation. The RAF had marked out four water runways with buoys and rubber tyres, and they were known as 'trots'; one was off the Lake near Hamworthy, the second extended along the Wareham Channel, with a third off Lilliput, and the fourth trot ran between Brownsea Island and Sandbanks. From Poole Harbour, BOAC would operate services to Portugal, South and West Africa, Egypt, India, Singapore, Australia and the USA, as well as special flights on behalf of the Air Ministry.

In *The Dorset Coast* Harry Ashley describes 'the great Sunderland flying boats dropping on the harbour like giant birds arriving from all corners of the world'. He was referring to the majestic Short 'C' Class 'Empire' flying boats, which had entered service with Imperial Airways in October 1936. They had originated out of the Empire Air Mail scheme

A fine shot of a Sunderland taking-off. (via J. Adams)

of 1935, whereby all mail between countries in the British Empire did not carry a surcharge. The airline's technical adviser, Major R. H. Mayo, drew up the specification and Short Brothers Ltd of Rochester were asked to design and build the aircraft. The demand for the new flying boat was such that Imperial Airways ordered a fleet of 28 at a total cost of £1¾ million (equivalent to about £44 million in today's values) straight off the drawing board, such was its faith in Arthur Gouge and his design team at Shorts. The airline's huge financial gamble paid off handsomely as the 'C' Class flying boat proved to be an outstanding success, and the design spawned the equally successful S.25 Sunderland military flying boat.

The first S.23 flying boat, which was designed to carry 24 passengers and 1½ tons of mail (later reduced to 17 passengers to carry more mail), made its initial flight in early July 1936, and within four months had made its first scheduled flight. The aircraft, named *Canopus* G-ADHL, became the flagship of the 'Empire' flying boat fleet and would complete over 2.8 million miles during its career. It was then the largest passenger-carrying monoplane in the country with a wing span of 114 feet, 88 feet long and an unladen weight of 10½ tons – a massive aircraft by the standards of the time. Powered by four 910 hp Bristol Pegasus XC radial engines, it had a top speed of 200 mph and a cruising speed of 164 mph with a range in excess of 800 miles. In total, 42 'C' Class 'Empire' flying boats were built with the later S.30 and S.33 modified models being even heavier and with a longer range, some capable of being refuelled in flight to give an operational range of 3,400 miles. Some of the 'Empire' flying boats operated with the Australian national airline, Qantas, and the Tasman Empire Airways Ltd, and during the war several served with the RAF.

It is quite amazing to consider that during the summer of 1940 whilst the Battle of Britain raged overhead, these 'Empire' flying boats slipped away from Poole Harbour for Cairo, Lagos, Durban, Karachi, Singapore and Sydney. The fall of France and the entry of Italy into the war meant that BOAC was forced to seek a new route to India and Australia, which became known as the 'Horseshoe Route', via Lagos through central and east Africa to Cairo, thence over Palestine and the Persian Gulf to India and beyond. On 4th/5th August Captain J. C. Kelly-Rogers, an ex-Merchant Navy man and Imperial Airlines pilot, left with S.30 *Clare* for the United States of America, the start of a regular wartime transatlantic

The Boeing 314 was the largest flying boat in the world. (National Air & Space Museum)

service. Ten days later *Clare* made its second crossing and amongst the passengers was Captain Harold Balfour, the Under-Secretary of State for Air, who was travelling to Washington to initiate the flying training programme for RAF pilots in the USA. Whilst he was there he heard of the possibility of purchasing three Boeing 314 'Clipper' flying boats, which he promptly bought for $1,050,000 *each* without any authority from the War Cabinet. On his return to this country Balfour found himself in particularly hot water with both Churchill and Lord Beaverbrook, the Minister of Aircraft Production, who felt that with the Battle of Britain at such a critical stage there were far more important priorities than buying such expensive flying boats. It was said that Beaverbrook refused to speak to Balfour for about eighteen months! Churchill told Balfour that his purchase 'has caused me a great deal of work and worry at a time when much else is happening.'

The three massive flying boats became known as 'Balfour Boeings'; the 314 was the largest flying boat in the world with a wing span of 152 feet, some 106 feet long and a take-off weight of 37½' tons! In July 1939 the 314A had inaugurated the first regular and scheduled passenger service across the Atlantic operated by Pan American World Airways, with luxurious accommodation for up to 74 daytime passengers or sleeping facilities for up to 40. From mid-1941 the three Boeings, named *Bristol*, *Berwick* and *Bangor* gave BOAC wonderful service flying over 4 million miles without an accident, and they were returned to the USA in 1948. In January 1942 Churchill, Lord Portal, Lord Beaverbrook and Admiral Pound all returned from Washington (via Bermuda) in *Berwick*, piloted by Captain Kelly-Rogers, in a smooth and trouble-free flight that took just under 18 hours. It was the first time that a British Prime Minister had flown the Atlantic, and all the VIPs were most impressed with the aircraft; even Lord Beaverbrook was won over and apologised to Captain Balfour.

Whilst BOAC's operations were continuing from Poole Harbour, almost unnoticed, in August 1940, a small Fleet Air Arm unit moved into the southern part of the harbour – on the north-west side of the Sandbanks peninsula. The unit was the basic Naval Seaplane Training School, which dated back to July 1917, and hitherto had operated from Calshot under the control of HMS *Daedalus*, a FAA shore base at Lee-on-Solent. The school trained FAA pilots in the basic techniques of seaplanes mainly to act as a reserve for the various catapult squadrons that operated from Naval vessels. The pilots would then pass onto Part II of the course, which was conducted at Lawrenny Ferry, also controlled by Lee-on-Solent. Shortly before the outbreak of the war, on 24th May 1939, the Seaplane Training School had become No 765 squadron. Unlike the RAF, the Navy gave all their training and support units squadron numbers. The FAA unit commandeered the premises of the Royal Motor Yacht Club, along with the club's small boat shed, which

Fairey Seafoxes operated from Sandbanks.

housed about fourteen small seaplanes. A small repair shed and a concrete ramp and slipway were the only other facilities provided for what was known to the locals as HMS *Tadpole* in sharp contrast to the big BOAC 'Empire' and Sunderland flying boats also using the Harbour; it was actually officially known as HMS *Daedalus II* (commissioned on 15th May 1940), although in late 1943 *Tadpole* became the official name of the station, when it then housed a pre-invasion Naval landing craft training unit.

The squadron, under the command of Lieutenant Commander L. B. Wilson, RN, operated a mixture of Supermarine Walruses, Fairey Swordfish and Seafoxes and a few Blackburn Rocs (only a few were fitted with floats to be flown as seaplanes). The Walrus was fondly known to all crews as the 'Shagbat' and was a single-engined amphibian. It had entered the Service in July 1936 and proved a most reliable and durable aircraft operating from vessels and shore bases as a spotter and reconnaissance aircraft. However, it probably gained even more wartime fame because of its air-sea rescue exploits with seven RAF squadrons operating in the United Kingdom. It is fondly remembered by many grateful airmen who were picked out of the 'drink' by this rather curious but unique aircraft, which calmly landed alongside them, even though they might be close to the enemy coast. The Mark I had a metal hull, but the Mark IIs were built of wood by Saunders-Roe Ltd on the Isle of Wight. When production of the Walrus finally ceased in January 1944 some 740 aircraft had been built.

The Swordfish dated from April 1934, and at the outbreak of the war this single-engined biplane looked decidedly obsolescent, with a top speed of just under 140 mph and its single forward firing machine gun. However, it proved to be a most versatile and effective aircraft, operating both as a land and seaplane, as a torpedo bomber, anti-U-boat aircraft, mine-layer, rocket projectile carrier and trainer. The nine Swordfish squadrons operated with rare distinction throughout the war, particularly in the Mediterranean; their action against the Italian fleet at Taranto in November 1940 has become legendary. Also it was in a torpedo-carrying Swordfish of No 825 (FAA) squadron that Lieutenant Commander Eugene Esmonde, DSO, was posthumously awarded the Victoria Cross in February 1942. Fondly dubbed the old 'Stringbag', it was one of the more remarkable and classic FAA aircraft of the Second World War with some 2,390 being built, and was the last biplane to fly

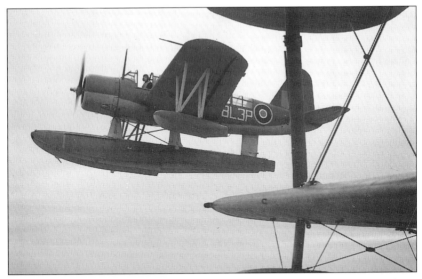

Vought-Sikorsky Kingfisher FN 678 'BL3P' of No 765 squadron, Sandbanks in 1943. (RAF Museum)

operationally, when retired from active service in 1953. There are still two airworthy examples, both with the Royal Naval Historical Flight at Yeovilton.

The Seafox was a small two-seat spotter and reconnaissance seaplane designed to be catapulted from cruisers. It was unusual inasmuch as the pilot sat in an open cockpit, whereas the observer/gunner was in an enclosed rear cockpit. The Seafox, first flown in May 1936, was planned to be equipped with a 500 hp Bristol Aquila engine but in fact was provided with a 395 hp Napier Rapier engine, which proved to be rather underpowered, and the Seafox cruised at just above 100 mph. Perhaps the aircraft's wartime fame resided in the famous naval action against the German battleship *Admiral Graf Spee* in December 1939 when a Seafox from HMS *Ajax* 'spotted' for the flotilla's guns – the first such occasion in World War II. Although production of the aircraft ceased in 1938, it remained in service until the summer of 1943, although by then it had been replaced by an American seaplane, the Vought-Sikorsky Kingfisher 1, a number of which would operate from Sandbanks from the summer of 1942.

BOAC's wartime operations were not without mishaps and losses. In the early hours of 11th May 1941 a Heinkel 111 attacked the harbour, and one of the bombs destroyed the Short S.21 *Mayo*, which had been converted to a S.30 'Empire'. This aircraft was the lower part of the remarkable and famous Short/Mayo composite, which had first flown in January 1938. The Heinkel was brought down by anti-aircraft fire, and only two of the crew survived. The top half of the composite, the small S.20 *Mercury* mail seaplane, did not survive its ex-partner very long, it was broken up by Shorts in the following August. The *Mercury*'s epic transatlantic flight in July 1938 had been by Imperial Airway's Captain D. C. T. Bennett, who became the Group Commander of Bomber Command's Pathfinder Force. Earlier in February S.30 *Clyde* had been destroyed beyond repair in a hurricane, and another 'Empire' boat, *Clare*, crashed in flames in the English Channel in September 1942 with the loss of 13 passengers and six crew. Then in late July 1943, one of the many Sunderlands seconded to BOAC crashed near Cloughan, County Kerry in Eire, when ten of the 25 on board were killed.

At the beginning of February 1941 another BOAC flying boat made its appearance at Poole, the American-built Consolidated Vultee PBY-5 Catalina, which had first flown in March 1935 and entered service with the US Navy in the following year. It was christened 'Catalina' by the RAF in 1939 when the first aircraft was received for flight trials, and this name would, in 1941, be officially adopted by the US Navy. The Catalina was a twin-engined maritime patrol and reconnaissance monoplane,

Consolidated PB-Y Catalina – both civil and Service Catalinas used Poole Harbour. (USAF)

powered by two 1,200 hp Pratt & Whitney Twin Wasp radial engines, which gave it a cruising speed of about 106 mph with an operational endurance of some 15½ hours. The aircraft would become famous for its wartime service with RAF Coastal Command from March 1941. Some 650 served in the Service and ultimately 18 squadrons were equipped with this very durable and reliable flying boat. The BOAC Catalina was named *Guba* and was planned for the Lisbon service and later another Catalina would be used on the West African service.

In the summer of 1942 RAF Coastal Command was heavily engaged in the Battle of the Atlantic, the long and bitter conflict with German U-boats. There was considerable pressure on their two main flying boat bases at Pembroke Dock and at Mount Batten, Plymouth, and Poole Harbour seemed an ideal location for another flying boat base, despite the strong presence of BOAC. Finally a location for the new RAF base was selected, about a mile or so to the west of Poole at Hamworthy on the northern side of Wareham Channel. Although there was insufficient available land for hangars and other ancillary buildings, RAF Poole came into service on 1st August. A week later it was renamed RAF Hamworthy.

At the end of the month No 461 (Royal Australian Air Force) squadron brought its nine Short S.25 Sunderland IIs from Mount Batten under the command of Squadron Leader G. R. Lovelock. The squadron had only been formed a few months earlier, and had been placed in No 19 (GR) Group of Coastal Command, which was commanded by Air Vice-Marshal G. R. Bromet, CB, CBE, DSO. This Group's operational remit was largely the Bay of Biscay, that area of sea that was so critical in the long running conflict against the German U-boats.

The Short Sunderland will forever epitomise Coastal Command in World War II, and it was, of course, a direct design development from the 'C' Class 'Empire' flying boats. The aircraft made its maiden flight on 16th October 1937 and the first production Sunderlands entered the Service in the following June, as the first monoplane flying boat. The Sunderland was the first British flying boat to feature power-operated gun turrets, and its strong defensive armament (seven/eight .303 machine guns) gained it the German nickname of 'Stachelschwein' or 'Flying Porcupine'. It was also able to carry up to 2,000 pounds of AS (Anti-submarine) bombs. The Mark IIs were powered by four 1,065 hp Bristol Pegasus XVIII engines, which allowed it to cruise at 115 mph

Short Sunderland of No 461 (RAAF) squadron.

with an endurance of 12½ hours. The Mark Vs had Pratt & Whitney engines, which increased the aircraft's top speed to 213 mph, and its endurance to 13½ hours. The Sunderland made its first U-boat kill in January 1940 and their crews would ultimately claim another 36 with more than 20 seriously damaged. The Mark IIs were equipped with ASV (Air to Surface Vessel) Mark II search radar.

By August 1945, 20 squadrons had been equipped with Sunderlands and when production ceased in June 1946 over 700 Sunderlands had been built. It was one of the most successful and long-serving of RAF aircraft and was not retired until May 1959. Lettice Curtis, an Air Transport Auxiliary pilot, one of the few women ATA pilots qualified to fly Sunderlands, considered it 'a delightful aeroplane, being light on the controls, and with its four engines and big keel surface, very manoeuvrable on the water'. It did, however, require more sheltered waters compared with the Catalina, which was unusually robust in rough water.

It is interesting to note in passing that it was estimated by the Air Ministry in late 1942 that the chances of Sunderland crews surviving one operational tour (800 hours) was 66%, compared with Catalina crews at 77½'%. It was stated that the 'wide difference' was mainly due 'to the longer average duration of operational sortie of the Catalina'. The

Catalina I had an endurance time of over 17 hours. As a rough comparison, the percentage for heavy and medium bomber crews was given as 44%, day fighter pilots as 43% but for torpedo bomber crews the figure was as low as 17½%!

The Sunderland crews operating from Hamworthy were almost fully engaged in making regular daylight patrols over the Bay of Biscay seeking out the elusive U-boats, although they were also employed on air/sea/rescue missions, and occasionally on anti-shipping patrols. On 12th August one of the squadron's Sunderlands, T9090, had been lost whilst on A/S/R duties and its twelve man crew were posted as missing. If the squadron's crews were operating at night they normally left from their previous base at Mount Batten, which had better night-landing facilities. The crews' patrols were most exacting and exhausting and they demanded precise navigation and utmost vigilance. There were, as one Coastal Command pilot later recalled, 'regular, monotonous hours of flying over unbounded sea, watching water with little to relieve the sheer drudgery – a constant need for alertness and concentration was required . . . 99% boredom interrupted by 1% heart-thumping action'. Although the crews made a total of eight attacks on U-boats during this period none were successful. It was estimated that it needed about 7,000 hours of flying time to destroy just one U-boat, hence why much of Coastal Command's patrols were 'water watching'! Unfortunately on 1st September one of the squadron's Sunderlands, T9113, was shot down in the Bay of Biscay by Junkers 88s.

The intolerable burdens carried by Coastal Command during the summer of 1942 were further increased during the autumn by Operation Torch, the Anglo-American invasion of French North Africa. Not only did the seven convoys leaving from Britain require air-cover but a Naval task force also required protection, and this was in addition to maintaining the U-boat offensive. The squadron's contribution to Operation Torch was to fly transport sorties to Gibraltar, providing supplies and airmen to service No 210 squadron operating from RAF New Base at Gibraltar. But towards the end of November the crews were back in action over the Bay of Biscay.

By the New Year the squadron's headquarters had moved into the Harbour Yacht Club at Lilliput and the pier at Salterns Way was extended, and its complement of Sunderlands increased to twelve; although one, T9085, failed to return on 21st January 1943. The level of

BOAC Sunderland being serviced at Poole Harbour. (British Airways via T. Harris)

U-boat sightings in the Bay of Biscay fell dramatically in January to less than ten in the month with no attacks being successful, and yet intelligence reports indicated that at least 45 U-boats would be crossing the Bay in the first two weeks of February; thus Operation Gondola was sanctioned on 4th February. This was the final operational decision of Air Chief Marshal Sir Philip B. Joubert de la Ferte, KCB, CMG, DSO, who, on 5th February, was replaced as AOC-in-C of Coastal Command by Air Marshal J. C. Slessor, CB, DSO, MC.

The operation was an intensive concentration of day/night patrols over a relatively small area of sea. The Sunderlands were allocated the inner section of the Bay, and 'Gondola' lasted for twelve days. It was followed in late March by 'Enclose I', a similar type of operation, which lasted for nine days, and although 26 sightings and 15 attacks were made, only one U-boat was destroyed. The day after 'Enclose I' started (21st March) a Sunderland, T9111, crashed into the mud-flats in the harbour. The aircraft was a write-off but all the crew managed to

115

survive. Two days later a BOAC Catalina – 'DA' – landing after a training flight crashed into flotsam and three of the crew were killed. Operation Enclose II was mounted from 6th to 13th April and eight days later the squadron's Sunderlands left Hamworthy for their new base at Pembroke Dock in west Wales, and in the following month were replaced by the Catalinas of No 210 squadron.

This squadron dated from February 1917 and since the formation of Coastal Command in 1936 it had operated with all the main RAF flying boats – Rangoon, Singapore, Sunderland (in June 1938) and Catalina (from April 1941). The squadron would have a most distinguished wartime career and besides operating from several British bases, it was also detached to north Russia, Gibraltar and Iceland. Its crews claimed eight U-boats in total, and one of its pilots, Flight Lieutenant J. A. Cruikshank, was awarded the Victoria Cross in July 1944, one of four won by Coastal Command airmen.

The squadron's Catalinas were equipped with Leigh lights, a powerful battery-operated searchlight, which was devised by Squadron Leader H. de Verde Leigh during late 1940 as a solution to the problems

Landing craft at Holes Bay. (Poole Museums Service)

encountered on night patrols. The Leigh light was first used for nocturnal anti-submarine patrols by Vickers Wellingtons in June 1942 and proved to be most successful. During the summer of 1943 it could be said that Coastal Command was beginning to win the battle of the Bay of Biscay; from the end of April to the beginning of August 26 U-boats were destroyed and another 17 damaged. The U-boat 'wolf packs' began using the coastal waters of north-west Spain between Ortegal and Finisterre. Coastal Command countered by introducing a series of regular patrols, 'A' to 'E', which were code-named 'Percussion', of which 'C' would involve No 210 squadron. A precise rectangular area of sea about 140 nautical miles to the north of Cape Finisterre and 80 miles to the west of the Cape was intensively patrolled at night. On 24th August a Catalina came to grief when returning from a training flight in heavy fog. It crashed at Round Island and only four of the twelve man crew survived. However, by the end of the year No 210 squadron moved away from the harbour, and by D-Day would be operating from Sullom Voe in the Shetlands. Indeed, on 7th May 1945, the squadron claimed the 196th and last U-boat sunk by aircraft of Coastal Command.

For the first time since the summer of 1940 there were no military aircraft operating from the harbour. In July 1943 (12th) 'W' Flight of No 700 FAA squadron was formed at Sandbanks with six Walruses and four

The plaque on the wall of the Old Custom House, Poole Harbour.

117

Swordfish for 'special duties' – to participate in the occupation of the Azores. However, within a fortnight the Flight had left for Macrihanish for ultimate service on HMS *Fencer*. In less than three months Sandbanks would close down. On 9th October the Seaplane Training School at Sandbanks had been placed on a care and maintenance basis, the need for this type of training having declined; No 765 squadron, now commanded by Lt Cdr L. D. Goldsmith, RNVR, was disbanded on the 25th of the month. However, Service flying would return to Poole Harbour when, on 13th January 1944, RAF Hamworthy was transferred into No 44 Group of Transport Command; the Command had been formed on 25th March 1943 from the existing three Groups and No 179 Wing in India. Thus RAF Sunderlands once again returned to the harbour, to commence ferrying mainly RAF aircrew and stores to India. At the end of April RAF Hamworthy was finally closed down, although RAF Sunderlands would return briefly to Poole in September 1945, bringing home repatriated prisoners from Japanese prisoner of war camps.

BOAC was forced to move its operations briefly to Pembroke Dock to leave the harbour free for the throng of landing craft and small vessels gathering there for Operation Overlord. J. Bolson & Son Ltd had been fully engaged in building assault landing craft, and in May some 60 rescue cutters of the US Coastguard moved into the harbour. The commemorative plaque on the wall of the Old Custom House on the Quay really says it all: 'On 5th June 1944 over 300 craft left the quays of Poole for the Normandy landings.'

The Corporation returned in September 1944 and on the 22nd of the month the respective Chiefs of the three British Services together with their entourages arrived at Poole in one of the Corporation's Boeings after attending the Ottawa Conference. By the end of March 1945 BOAC had 160 aircraft in service including 42 flying boats, and during the war its crews had flown more than 55 million miles, carrying over 271,000 passengers and over 48 million pounds of cargo and mail. The Corporation would continue to operate its flying boats from Poole for another three years, before it moved its operations back to Hythe in Southampton Water at the end of March 1948; but by then the days of the grand and stately flying boats were fast coming to an end. In November 1950 their operations ceased, thus bringing to a close a most remarkable and very successful chapter of British aviation history, in which Poole Harbour featured prominently.

4

HENSTRIDGE

One of the longest and most acrimonious disputes of the inter-war years, between the Air Ministry and the Admiralty, concerned the control of those aircraft and pilots serving on Naval aircraft carriers and vessels. It all dated back to the end of the First World War when the Royal Naval Air Service had been handed over to the Air Ministry to become an integral part of the newly formed RAF. Some Service historians considered the long running argument to be nothing more than 'a storm in a teapot', but nevertheless it did engage the two Service chiefs – Lord Trenchard and Admiral Beatty – in quite furious debate, which continued between the two Services long after they had both retired.

Since April 1924 the airmen serving with, and on, Naval vessels had been in the Fleet Air Arm (FAA) of the Royal Air Force. However, on 21st July 1937, under the recommendation of Sir Thomas Inskip, the Minister for the Co-ordination of Defence, the FAA was transferred to the control of the Admiralty. The change was to take place within two years and all personnel would be Naval. At the time, and for a number of years afterwards, this political decision was considered by the Air Staff to be 'disastrous', and a body blow for the expanding RAF. It would be fair to say that neither Naval aircraft nor aircraft carriers gained much validity with the Admiralty and their senior officers afloat, until the Battle of Taranto in November 1940, when FAA aircraft made such a contribution to the ultimate defeat of the Italian battle fleet. The actual transfer of the FAA took place in May 1939 when eight RAF bases were handed over to the Admiralty. From this political ruling of 1937 the airfield at Henstridge indirectly owes its inception.

Before the outbreak of the war the Air Ministry Aerodromes Board offered the Admiralty some 13 sites they considered suitable for development into airfields according to the Admiralty's criteria. Perhaps Yeovilton was the most famous Royal Naval Air Station to be developed from these sites, although three (Ibsley, Holmsley South and Hartfordbridge Flats) later became RAF airfields. Included in the list of sites were Fifehead Magdalen and Styles Farm. The latter, situated in Somerset but almost on the boundary with Dorset, was ultimately developed as Henstridge, and in fact Styles Farmhouse would become the station headquarters. Whether Fifehead Magdalen was considered to be a separate site is not very clear, as that village is less than two miles to the east of Henstridge airfield.

Construction work on the 355 acre site about 1½ miles to the north-east of Henstridge village did not begin until August 1941 and it would be another 20 months before it was considered ready for occupation, which appeared to be a rather long drawn out process, at least compared with RAF airfields built during the same time. It should be noted that the Admiralty airfield programme was completely separate to that of the Air Ministry, and one of the reasons for the delay was that the Admiralty's share of construction labour allocated by the Government was already heavily involved in building Naval shore bases and installations. Furthermore Naval aviation was always fairly low on the Admiralty's list of priorities.

Wartime airfields specially constructed for the FAA had several different features from those of the RAF. They were usually provided with four (instead of three) runways, normally three at 1,000 yards and a fourth one at 100 yards longer, and the runways were 30 yards wide instead of the more usual 50 yards; the smaller dimensions were considered entirely adequate for the relatively small aircraft operated by the FAA. In most cases the runways were constructed of tarmac laid on hardcore, rather than of concrete. The control towers were materially different, three storeys instead of the RAF's two, with a large glasshouse superimposed on the top, which afforded an excellent view of the airfield. Frequently the hangars were different. The Admiralty designed their own special hangars and most of the buildings on FAA airfields were Nissen huts of various sizes and spans, rather than the brick and concrete-rendered huts, which were so prevalent on RAF airfields. Of course it must be borne in mind that the majority of FAA airfields were used for training as the *raison d'être* of the FAA was to operate with the Navy at sea. Indeed the precept for Naval aviation had been set by Admiral Beatty back in the First World War, which was that the Navy wanted sailors who could fly, rather than pilots who happened to be in the Navy.

It has already been noted that Henstridge along with Arbroath were the only wartime airfields (RAF included) to be provided with five runways. Both these airfields included an imitation carrier deck for ADDLS (Aeroplane Dummy Deck Landings). Henstridge had always been designed to serve as an operational flying training airfield, one of 27

RNAS Henstridge – HMS Dipper *– from the air, October 1945. (Fleet Air Arm Museum)*

FAA training airfields that were built during the war. The rapid expansion of the FAA, which was planned to increase from some 2,300 aircraft in June 1942 to over 6,300 aircraft of all types by the end of 1943, ensured that such training airfields would be at a premium, and in fact the RAF was forced to hand over a number of its airfields to the Admiralty, as well as offering 'lodger' facilities to a number of FAA squadrons.

Henstridge was commissioned on 1st April 1943 as HMS *Dipper*, with a maximum capacity of 120 aircraft. It was then common Naval practice to name RNAS shore establishments after bird's names – Yeovilton was HMS *Heron* – but with perhaps the notable exception of Lee-on-Solent, which was HMS *Daedalus*. As Henstridge was allocated to be the training airfield for nearby Yeovilton, its first squadron arrived from that station, No 761, which was in effect No 2 Naval Air Fighter School. The squadron was equipped with a mixture of aircraft – Fairy Fulmars, Supermarine Spitfire Vs, Seafire 1bs and Miles Masters. The marking of aircraft differed from the RAF. In January 1943 a letter was allocated to all its shore bases, thus Henstridge was 'G' and the squadron's aircraft bore codes from 'G1' to 'G6'. Although the airfield was provided with 'Dummy Deck' runways, the escort carrier HMS *Ravager* was also used for deck landing training.

The Fulmar was just one of a number of aircraft that Fairey Aviation

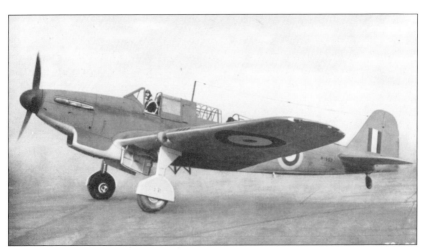

Fairey Fulmar: originally the FAA's equivalent to the Spitfire.

Co Ltd had developed for the Navy – including the Fox, Seafox, Albacore and Swordfish. It had emerged from an Air Ministry specification P4/34 for a high-performance fighter to operate from aircraft carriers, and was intended to replace the FAA's rather antiquated biplanes. Although the original prototype had flown in January 1937, the first Fulmars did not enter the Service until June 1940. It was a two-seat carrier-based fighter (the Navy felt that a navigator was essential for fighters), and was armed with eight .303 inch machine guns, the first time a FAA fighter had been so heavily armed. The Fulmar was then considerd to be 'the FAA's equivalent to the Spitfire'. The aircraft served the FAA well until it was superseded by the Fairey Firefly and the ubiquitious Seafire. In February 1943 the last of some 600 Fulmars was delivered to the FAA and they then became increasingly used as trainers, although they were still flying operationally in early 1945. The first production Fulmar, N1854, is on display at the Fleet Air Arm Museum at Yeovilton.

The Seafire was, of course, the Naval version of the Spitfire, which had been adapted for carrier operations. As equally successful as its twin, the Seafire proved to be the salvation of the FAA from late 1942 onwards, and they survived into the immediate post-war years with one Seafire squadron operating in June 1950 in the Korean War. The following year they were phased out of frontline service but remained with RNVR training units until late 1954. Henstridge would house a veritable host of Seafires at any given time, and the sight and sounds of this doughty aircraft became most familiar to the local communities. The Mark Is were converted from Spitfire Vs, whereas the Mark IIs and IIIs were built as Seafires with the latter Mark being the first to be constructed with folding wings, hinged inboard of the cannons with the wing tips folding downwards – the so-called 'praying mantis' wings. This enabled the aircraft to be moved on aircraft carrier lifts and it afforded easier deck handling. The Mark IIIs were the most prolific, with 1,220 being built from November 1943 to July 1945 in three versions, 'F', fighter, 'L', low-altitude fighter, and 'LR', low-altitude reconnaissance.

The School had in excess of 100 aircraft at Henstridge, including the Miles Masters, which were advanced trainers that had handling characteristics similar to those of the Hurricane and Spitfire, and were probably the best designed single-engined advanced aircraft of their day. The aircraft was provided with a sliding canopy and gave student

123

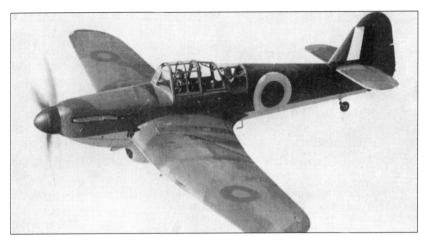

Miles Master 1: an advanced trainer.

pilots a taste for high-speed flying. The first Master had flown in March 1939 but just a handful had entered the Service by the outbreak of the war. The Master had a maximum speed of some 240 mph, and an initial rate of climb of 2,000 feet per minute. It proved to be a most reliable trainer with over 2,000 being produced. All were provided with an instructor's seat in the rear cockpit, which could be raised to give better vision over the head of the pupil in front. The Master could also be adapted to tow gliders, and led directly to the Martinet, the RAF's first specially designed target tower.

The School's Chief Flying Instructor was Lieutenant Commander Richard J. 'Dickie' Cork, DSO, DFC, or 'Corkie', who had joined the Navy in early 1939 and had been loaned to the RAF in June 1940, when he flew Hurricanes with No 242 squadron (commanded by Douglas Bader) in the Battle of Britain. Cork claimed five victories and was awarded the DFC, which was later converted to a DSC by the Admiralty. He had gained no small fame when flying off the carrier HMS *Indomitable* engaged in escorting a Malta convoy; Cork shot down no less than six enemy aircraft in a day. He remained in command of the squadron until the middle of November but sadly he would be killed in a flying accident in 1944 whilst serving in Burma.

The airfield was further developed during 1943 with the establishment of an aircraft repair depôt at Gibbs Marsh Farm, followed

124

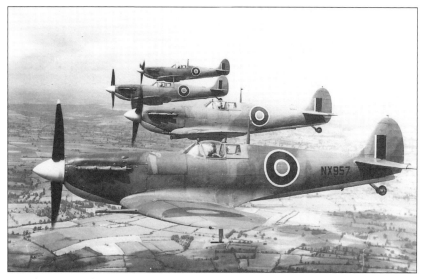

Lt Cdr R. J. Cork, DSO, DSC, with Seafires of No 761 squadron, No 2 NAFS. (Fleet Air Arm Museum)

in October by the opening of 'B' camp at Prior's Down due south of the airfield and close to Stalbridge. Both of these sites were actually in Dorset. It was during October that No 894 squadron, which had been serving on HMS *Illustrious*, was re-equipped with Seafire IIIs, and along with No 887 squadron formed a new Wing – 24th Naval Fighter – which in January 1944 moved away to Burscough or HMS *Ringtail* near Liverpool. The airfield would play host to a number of FAA squadrons, one of the earliest to use the facilities, No 794, a Naval Air Firing Unit, arriving towards the end of November for a brief stay. It departed during the following month for Charlton Horethorpe, which was another FAA training airfield in Somerset sited some six miles to the north-west. In February 1944 No 748 squadron arrived from St Merryn, HMS *Vulture* in Cornwall. The squadron had been formed in October 1942 as a Fighter Pool, No 10 Naval Operational Training Unit, for Seafire pilots, and it remained at Henstridge for about five weeks before leaving for Yeovilton. Another squadron arrived from St Merryn, No 736, which was part of the School of Air Combat formed at that airfield in the previous September. The School inculcated the techniques of air

Barracudas of No 736 squadron at Henstridge. (Fleet Air Arm Museum)

combat in experienced Naval fighter pilots. This squadron's arrival saw the first appearance at Henstridge of yet another famous Fairey aircraft used by the FAA – the Barracuda.

The aircraft dated back to 1937 and was intended to be the replacement for the Fairey Swordfish and Albacore biplanes. It was designed to be used in the dive and torpedo bomber/reconnaissance role. The Barracuda first flew in December 1940, making its first deck landing six months later, but it did not enter the FAA until January 1943. However, within a year there were twelve Barracuda squadrons in service. It was a rather aggressive aircraft in appearance with a high wing design along with a similarly high brace to its tailplane. The aircraft's powerful Rolls-Royce Merlin 32 engine gave it a top speed close to 240 mph, and it could carry either six 250 pound bombs or four 450 pound depth charges, or one 1,620 pound torpedo. Carrying a three man crew the Barracudas gained a certain celebrity for their long and concentrated attacks on the German battleship *Tirpitz* during April 1944.

During late 1943 the Admiralty was requested by the Air Ministry to 'loan' some FAA squadrons to both Coastal Command and the 2TAF for Operation Overlord. Amongst its responses was the decision, in February 1944, to disband Nos 808, 885, 886 and 897 squadrons and then reform them as No 3 Naval Fighter Wing at Lee-on-Solent to become the gunnery observation force for the heavy guns of the Royal Navy. The Wing would be placed in the Air Spotting Pool of No 34 Reconnaissance

126

Wing of 2TAF and would operate until the middle of July from Lee-on-Solent. Nos 808 and 897 were equipped with Spitfire L Mk Vbs, whereas the other two squadrons would operate with Seafire L Mk IIIs. In total the Wing would comprise 42 aircraft with some 60 pilots on complement.

The Spitfire LVcs were perhaps just about beginning to show their age, and most of the 2TAF's Spitfire squadrons were operating Mark IXs. The Spitfire V had first entered Fighter Command in March 1941 and it proved to be the most numerous of all Marks with over 6,400 being produced. The 'L' version had clipped wings and a Rolls-Royce Merlin 45M engine, armed with a mixture of cannons and machine guns, with the provision to carry either 250 or 500 pound bombs. The Spitfires and Seafires arrived at Henstridge in early March for their pilots to practise and hone their low-flying and attack procedures and techniques, but by the end of the month the Wing had moved back to Lee-on-Solent. On D-Day pilots from No 897 claimed an early victim, a Me 109 destroyed, as well as attacking a German midget submarine. For the short period of time the Wing was training at Henstridge, the airfield was literally crowded with aircraft, its busiest period of the war.

The Naval Air Fighter School received an addition to its complement in June, when No 718 squadron was formed at Henstridge to undertake the training of pilots for Army Co-operation operations. The squadron was inevitably equipped with Seafires but also it was provided with a few Spitfire PR XIIIs for low-level photographic sorties with its three F24 cameras – two for vertical shots and one for oblique. This camera had been introduced in 1925 and remained in use in the RAF for 30 years. It could also be hand-held, and although excellent for low or medium level photography, the camera lacked the focal length for high-altitude photography, hence why the F52 camera was introduced in 1942. No 718 squadron would be redesignated the School of Naval Air Reconnaissance in April 1945, and four months later it would move out to Ballyherbert in Northern Ireland, an ex-RAF airfield.

Henstridge had became the FAA's major training base for Seafire pilots, most of which would be transferred for service in the Far East; in early 1945 there were still eight FAA squadrons equipped with Seafire IIIs flying from six aircraft carriers in the Pacific. As the Spitfires changed from Merlin to Rolls-Royce Griffon engines, it followed that Seafires would also be re-engined. Thus the Seafire XV entered the FAA with No 802 squadron in May 1945, although too late to see any operational service. The new Griffon powered Seafires did, however, manage to prolong the life of the Naval Air Fighter School until January 1946 when No 761 squadron, under the command of Lt Cdr P. N. Charlton, DFC, RN, was disbanded on the 16th, with its remaining aircraft and personnel absorbed into No 759 squadron at Yeovilton. HMS *Dipper* was decommissioned on 11th October 1946, although the airfield still remained a satellite of Yeovilton. After some training activity during the mid-1950s, the airfield was finally closed to Service flying in June 1957.

The airfield was used during the 1950s by the helicopters of Air Whaling and later Bristow Helicopters, but it was not until the 1970s that Henstridge began to be used by private light aircraft. The airfield is still used for private flying with a single resurfaced tarmac runway of some 820 yards, which includes a refurbished concrete 'Dummy Deck'. At the time of writing (Spring 1999) there are a number of special 'fly-ins' planned, and there is an active association known as 'Friends of Henstridge Airfield'.

5

HURN

Hurn has been operating as an airfield continuously since 1941, and over that passage of time it has witnessed a vast array of military and civil aircraft using its runways and facilities, from tiny biplanes right up to large modern jetliners. And yet the airfield's origins might have been at least ten years earlier, if only the Bournemouth Council had decided to act upon Sir Alan Cobham's strong recommendations that the site at West Parley afforded excellent potential for development as a municipal aerodrome. However, it was left to the Air Ministry Aerodromes Board, ten years later, to recognise the value of the site, which was situated on a gravel plain between the rivers Moors and Stour about four miles to the north-northeast of Bournemouth.

Building work commenced in the winter of 1940 and the completed airfield was planned to be a Fighter Command station, tentatively allocated as a satellite for nearby Ibsley, which was also in the throes of construction and would open in April 1941. The Luftwaffe had certainly taken note of the construction work at Hurn, because in the early evening of 3rd December five high explosive bombs and a number of incendiaries were dropped, but they caused very little damage and barely hindered the building work. The severe winter of 1940/1 would cause far more delay!

It was not until the summer of 1941 that the airfield was ready for occupation. Its three tarmac runways at 5,200, 4,800 and 3,400 feet awaited their first aircraft. However, it could now be said that the priorities of the Air Ministry had subtly changed, and the airfield's immediate wartime future would lie in its use as a transport base. For this reason, in the following year, the airfield's facilities would be further enhanced with two of its runways being lengthened to 6,000 and 3,900 feet respectively and resurfaced with concrete, able to take the heaviest aircraft in service. A perimeter road and an increased number of hard standings were laid, along with the provision of extra hangarage space. Ultimately Hurn would become one of the best equipped wartime airfields in the country, with 56 hard standings of various sizes and no less than 17 hangars, the majority being of the Blister type.

On 1st August 1941 Wing Commander G. K. Horner of the Special Duty Flight at Christchurch formally took over the airfield on behalf of the RAF, pending the arrival of the appointed Station Commander, Group Captain P. J. R. King, 18 days later. He and the Flight's pilots would have made a number of trial landings and take-offs to ensure that the runways were satisfactory, which was the standard Service procedure before an airfield was accepted from the contractors. With one of those strange quirks of fate it was in fact a fighter aircraft that first used the runways at Hurn. A Westland Whirlwind of No 263 squadron, based at Filton, made an emergency landing on 6th August after being damaged in combat with Me 109s over Cherbourg.

One week later (the 13th) the Telecommunications Flying Unit arrived from Middle Wallop; the Unit would undertake flight trials for the scientists working at the Telecommunications & Research Establishment at Worth Matravers. It had a complement of over 50 aircraft - a rare selection of machines covering the whole spectrum of Service aviation, from Tiger and Hornet Moth biplanes, fighters such as Havocs, Defiants, Spitfires, Hurricanes and Beaufighters to the light and heavy bombers, Blenheims, Wellingtons and Halifaxes. Then in the second week of November (the 10th) the Special Duty Flight finally vacated Christchurch, and moved into Hurn.

Perhaps one of the most far-reaching and important experimental flights conducted by the Unit during the spring of 1942 was the trialling of H2S – a centimetric wavelength airborne radar. A rotating scanner mounted in a perspex blister under the aircraft's fuselage transmitted radar signals to the ground over which the aircraft was flying, and the echoes were returned to display a shadowy image of the ground passing below over a ten mile radius, onto a cathode ray set (or Plan Position

Indicator) on board. The device's unusual codename is the chemical formula for the noxious gas, hydrogen sulphide, and it was said to have originated from 'It stinks!', Professor F. A. Lindemann's retort to the boffins' excuse for its tardy development; Lindemann, later Lord Cherwell, was the Prime Minister's Scientific Adviser. The Unit had been supplied with a Halifax Mark 2 srs 1 – V9977 – built under contract by English Electric and specially adapted to take the H2S equipment. It trialled the new device over Bournemouth and Poole at an altitude of 8,000 feet. H2S was first used operationally by the Pathfinder Force on 30th/31st January 1943, and subsequently by the rest of Bomber Command. The H2S sets were manufactured locally, in a factory at West Howe.

In January 1942 a detachment of No 1425 Communications Flight arrived at the airfield from Honeybourne in Worcestershire with a handful of Consolidated Liberator IIs. The Flight operated in Ferry Command, which had been formed on 18th July 1941 under the command of Air Chief Marshal Sir Frederick W. Bowhill, KCB, CMG, DSO, late of Coastal Command. It was almost exclusively engaged in flying courier services to the Middle East and Africa, and by the end of March some 500 flights had left Hurn. The Liberator, as a B-24 heavy bomber, served with distinction in the Eighth Air Force. However, the first Liberators had entered the RAF in mid-1941 and because of the aircraft's long operational range they had been placed in Coastal Command. The Mark IIs did not have a USAAF equivalent, and 139 were produced specially to the order of the Air Ministry; probably the most famous was AL504 *Commando*, the interior of which was equipped to a high VIP standard, and it became the personal transport aircraft for Winston Churchill. By July this aircraft was hangared and serviced at Hurn along with a number of other 'VIP' aircraft.

No 1425 Flight would remain at Hurn until 26th July before moving away to Lyneham in Wiltshire, which was fast becoming the RAF's main transport base, as it is indeed to the present day. It is interesting to note in passing that Wing Commander Donald C. Bennett was at Hurn on 4th July 1942 preparing to take his Halifax squadron, No 10, to the Middle East for operations in support of the North African campaign. However, he was called back urgently to Bomber Command Headquarters and offered the command of the new Pathfinder Force, which was officially formed in August. After the war Bennett would again return to civil aviation and, of course, to Hurn.

Armstrong Whitworth Whitley Vs of No 77 squadron. Both Nos 296 and 297 squadrons operated Whitley Vs.

Towards the end of May the TRE Flight had left for Defford because its parent establishment at Worth Matravers had been evacuated to a more secure location at Great Malvern. Hurn would now become closely involved with the development of airborne forces, both glider-borne and by parachute. On 1st June the control of the airfield was placed under No 38 Wing of the Army Co-operation Command, and on that day Air Marshal Sir Arthur S. Barratt, KCB, CMG, MC, the AOC-in-C, visited Hurn to inspect his Command's new airfield. Sir Arthur was a most experienced officer, who had commanded the RAF squadrons in France during 1940, and was well versed in army support tactics. Barratt was one of the most popular RAF senior commanders, his airmen, perhaps a little unkindly, had dubbed him 'Ugly'!

No 38 Wing had been formed on 15th January 1942 expressly to provide transport support for 1st Parachute Brigade, although initially its main preoccupation would be with training. However, the Group was also tasked to develop the techniques of towing gliders and the accurate dropping of paratroops. The Wing was based at Netheravon and commanded by Group Captain (later Air Commodore) Sir Nigel Norman, who sadly would be killed in May 1943 whilst en route to North Africa to set up the Wing's advance base for the airborne invasion of Sicily. Initially No 38 Wing comprised just two squadrons, No 296, which was known as the 'Glider experience' squadron, and No 297 delegated as the 'Parachute exercise' squadron. It was the latter that arrived at Hurn on 5th June with its Whitley Vs.

The Armstrong Whitworth A.W.38 Whitley had first flown in March 1936 and entered the Service twelve months later; its name was taken from the district of Coventry where the factory was situated. The Whitley was a rather cumbersome inelegant aircraft, often referred to as 'The Flying Barn Door'! However, Whitleys were the first to drop leaflets over Germany in September 1939. They also made the first bombing raid over Germany in March 1940 and over Italian targets the following June, as well as transporting the first paratroops into action over Southern Italy in February 1941. The Whitleys had been withdrawn from Bomber Command in the spring of 1942, but they gained a new lease of life as both paratroop carriers and glider-tugs, and also with Coastal Command.

The Whitleys were joined later by North American Mustang Is of No 170 (AC) squadron, which earlier in the month had been formed at Weston Zoyland. This aircraft owed its origins to an order by the British Air Purchasing Commission in America, and had first flown in September 1940 designated by the company as the P-51. From the outset the aircraft looked an outright winner; it had clean fine lines, an ideal cockpit layout, good performance and unusually squared wings. The Air Ministry immediately placed an order for 320, but Service trials showed that although the aircraft had an impressive performance at low-altitudes, this tended to fall away sharply at higher altitudes. Thus the Mustang did not really fit the bill for bomber escort duties, and it was relegated to army support duties; although in October 1943 it was the first single-engined RAF fighter to fly over Germany during a raid on the Dortmund-Ems Canal. Of course the aircraft's salvation came with the experiment of replacing its under-powered and 'asthmatic' Allison engine with a Rolls-Royce/Packard Merlin, when it developed into one of the classic pursuit fighters of the Second World War.

In the following month the other Whitley squadron, No 296, also moved in from Netheravon and both squadrons began undertaking paratroop exercises over Salisbury Plain. During July there were six Airspeed Horsa gliders at Netheravon undergoing intensive loading and towing trials, and the Wing had plans to supply 30 Horsas to each of their airfields by the end of September. The Glider Pilot Regiment, which had been officially formed in February 1942, already had well in excess of 400 trained glider pilots, who would begin conversion training to Horsas in July; all were Army personnel but had been trained by the RAF instructors on the General Aircraft's Hotspurs. The immediate plan was that by September, the two Whitley squadrons would begin full scale training exercises towing the Horsas. Unfortunately, during loading test flights undertaken in August, it was discovered to great consternation that the Whitley lacked sufficient power to tow a fully laden Horsa. Further trials and urgent discussions continued through September but they led to only one conclusion, the more powerful four-engined bombers – the Stirling and Halifax – would have to be used as glider-tugs, and the AOC-in-C of Bomber Command, Air Chief Marshal Sir Arthur Harris, was not happy that he might lose some of his heavy bombers. Thus during October the crews of the two Whitley squadrons found themselves engaged on leaflet-dropping operations or 'Nickelling' (to use the code-name) over Paris, Lille and Northern France. However, by the 25th of the month all three squadrons had left Hurn, Nos 297 and 170 to Thruxton and No 296 to Andover.

The location of Hurn, along with its facilities, made it an ideal airfield from which to mount Operation Cackle. This involved the movement of USAAF aircraft and airmen, who had been transferred to the US Twelfth Air Force, to Gibraltar and North Africa, to take part in Operation Torch – the combined Allied invasion of North Africa. Lieutenant General Luther W. Sweetser Jr arrived at Hurn to mastermind the move, and for the next month or so the airfield would be swamped with American aircraft and personnel.

On 3rd November the first six B-17Fs (Flying Fortresses) of 97th Bomb Group arrived to transport American and British commanders and senior officers to Gibraltar, amongst them Generals Dwight D. Eisenhower and Mark Clarke, his deputy. Five B-17s left Hurn for warmer climes on the 5th, with another taking-off the following day. The 97th, which was based at Polebrook in Northamptonshire, was then the most famous Bomb Group in the USAAF, because, on 17th August, it had launched the Eighth Air Force's first heavy bombing mission of the war. In September the Group, along with 301st (Heavy) Bomb Group at Chelveston, had been allocated to serve with the Twelfth Air Force in the Mediterranean. One of the 97th's Squadron Commanders, Major Paul L. Tibbets, would pilot the B-29 *Enola Gay* that dropped the first atomic bomb on Hiroshima.

Also on 3rd November the first American C-47s arrived at Hurn to transport supplies and troops to Gibraltar. The Douglas C-47 (Skytrain, or universally known as Dakota) became the best known transport aircraft of all time. It was the 'work-horse' of the USAAF, able to carry two tons of freight or 20 fully equipped troops, and was the military version of the successful DC-3 airliner. C-47s were fondly dubbed by American servicemen as the 'Gooney Birds'! The first British Dakotas would not arrive in the United Kingdom until February 1943, when a number went to BOAC, but the majority operated with Coastal and Transport Commands; at the end of the war the RAF had almost 1,500 Dakotas on complement. The aircraft would be equally successful operating in the post-war years with many commercial airlines (including BOAC) and countless cargo companies worldwide, over 20,000 of all versions being produced, making it perhaps the most successful aircraft of all time. During Operation Cackle over 100 C-47s, in total, left Hurn, along with 57 B-17s, the last leaving on the 28th of the month. The 'Torch' landings took place on 8th November and a month later the transport of supplies and men was complete. It had been conducted most efficiently and effectively, without a single incident.

B-17 Peggy D *of 97th Bomb Group. During November 1942 57 B-17s left Hurn for North Africa.*

135

Armstrong Whitworth Albemarle, V1823, of No 297 squadron.

The final departure of the American airmen from Hurn witnessed the return of the Army Co-operation squadrons. Mustang 1s of No 239 squadron moved in from Odiham for about a month's stay, followed by the Whitley Vs of No 297 with a number of Horsa gliders. A special Gunnery Flight, No 1498 (Target Towing), was formed at the airfield, which would provide air-firing practice for the two squadrons. The Flight was equipped with Westland Lysanders and Miles M.25 Martinets, the latter being the RAF's first specially designed target-tug. Also during the month a small number of Fairey Swordfish IIs of Nos 811 and 816 (FAA) squadrons were detached from Thorney Island, to patrol the English Channel seeking German E-boats. In the New Year No 3 Overseas Aircraft Despatch Unit was formed at Hurn to prepare aircraft and crews for flights to the Middle East delivering Wellingtons, Halifaxes and later Liberators. Perhaps an early indication of the future use of the airfield in the immediate post-war years?

Towards the end of January 1943 a new aircraft arrived at Hurn, the Armstrong Whitworth A.W.41 Albemarle. This aircraft had originally been designed by the Bristol Aeroplane Company, as a twin-engined medium bomber (known as Type 155) back in 1938, and it was intended to replace the Wellington. However, the final design and development of the aircraft was transferred to Armstrong Whitworth. The first prototype was constructed of tubular steel and compressed wood, and it was provided with a tricycle undercarriage of American design, which in those days was a quite advanced concept. The first prototype flew in 1939 but subsequently crashed and the second one was not ready until March 1940, some ten months late, as there were already production orders for 1,000 Albemarles, scheduled to be completed by November 1940. Repeated changes in the production lines at A. W. Hawksley Ltd, the main producer, due to an increasing number of modifications, seriously delayed the aircraft's delivery to the Service. The Albemarle was found to be greatly underpowered with its sole armament being a four-gun dorsal turret, and in many respects the aircraft was inferior to the Wellington, the bomber it was intended to replace! The development programme had already cost over £6 million, and yet the aircraft was said to have 'no future as a bomber'. It was then discovered that by cutting a hole in the fuselage floor, the aircraft could be used to carry ten paratroopers. In the autumn of 1942 the Albemarle's role was confirmed as a long distance transport and troop carrier, and in the following February it was approved to tow Horsa gliders, thus replacing Whitley Vs.

No 296 squadron was the first to be re-equipped with Albemarles, and it was planned to convert the other two squadrons when enough crews had completed their conversion training at No 42 Operational Training Unit at Hampstead Norris. On the night of 9th/10th February Albemarles from No 296 dropped leaflets over Rouen, and then on 17th April two Albermarle crews left Hurn for a bombing raid over France – five years after the aircraft had been designed for that very purpose!

The airfield was now heavily engaged in preparing for Operation Husky – the invasion of Sicily and the first to include major airborne troop landings. The RAF's contribution to the landings was code-named 'Beggar' and the Army's 'Turkey Buzzard' – one can only speculate on how and why some of the wartime code-names were chosen! No 1 Heavy Glider Maintenance Unit was formed at Hurn to prepare the Horsa gliders for their long transport flight to North Africa, and a detachment of airmen from No 13 Maintenance Unit arrived from Henlow in Bedfordshire to make the necessary modifications to Halifax Vs into glider-tugs, as well as preparing them for the long flight; this involved fitting extra fuel tanks and removing the dorsal turrets to lighten the aircraft. It was 'A' Flight of No 295 squadron, under the command of Squadron Leader A. M. B. Wilkinson, that would tow the gliders some 1,300 miles to North Africa.

The crews of the Albemarle squadron began training on the use of 'Rebecca', which was an airborne radar directional air/ground device working in conjunction with 'Eureka' – a ground beacon. The radar impulses transmitted by the Rebecca apparatus were returned by Eureka as directional 'blips' on the navigator's grid screen, thus providing fairly accurate fixes on the dropping zones. In early June (the 3rd) the Halifaxes with their Horsa gliders in tow left Hurn for Portreath in Cornwall and they would be followed by No 296's Albemarles, which would be principally used to tow the American Waco CG-4 gliders. The airborne invasion of Sicily, in early July, was really a disaster. Of the 137 gliders released, 69 landed in the rough sea, and 56 scattered on landing. Only 12 found the landing zone! The paratroops fared little better, only about 5% were effective. It was not until the autumn that the two squadrons arrived back at Hurn.

On its return No 295 squadron was re-equipped with Albemarles, its Halifaxes being transferred to No 298 squadron at Tarrant Rushton, the nearby airfield which had opened earlier in May. Then, in November, a new squadron, No 590, was formed at Hurn, also equipped with Albemarles. No 38 Wing had been constituted as a Group, with effect from 15th October, and Air Vice-Marshal L. N. Hollinghurst, CB, OBE, DFC, placed in command. The Group's squadrons would now be fully involved in a range of training exercises in preparation for Operation Overlord. In the meantime, in February 1944 all three Albemarle squadrons were engaged on dropping arms and supplies for Special Operations Executive (SOE) agents and Resistance fighters in France to assist the two regular 'Special Duties' squadrons, Nos 138 and 161 operating from Tempsford in Bedfordshire, who were unable to cope with the seemingly insatiable demand for arms and supplies as the date of the invasion neared. However, on 14th March Hurn was transferred to No 11 Group of the Air Defence of Great Britain, and the three squadrons left for their D-Day bases – Nos 295 and 570 to Harwell and No 296 to Brize Norton. The airfield would now, if only for a relatively brief period, become what it was originally intended for, back in 1940 – a fighter station, although on a number of occasions several fighter squadrons, both RAF and USAAF, had used the airfield as a temporary advanced base whilst engaged on escorting USAAF heavy bombers over France.

On 17th March the first Hawker Typhoon 1Bs began to arrive at Hurn in some numbers. They belonged to No 143 Wing of No 83 Group of the 2TAF, and comprised three Royal Canadian Air Force squadrons, which had all been formed 'at Bournemouth' during the previous four months.

Wing Commander R. T. P. Davidson, DFC, the Canadian Commander of No 143 (RCAF) Wing beside his Typhoon with his initials 'RD'. (Bournemouth International Airport via Mike Phipp)

The Wing was commanded by Wing Commander R. T. P. Davidson, DFC, of RCAF. Davidson would be shot down over France in May, but he evaded capture and worked with the French Resistance. No 438 (Wild Cat) and No 439 (Westmount) squadrons had already converted to Typhoons, whereas No 440 (City of Ottawa and Beaver) was a Hurricane squadron, but would convert to Typhoons before the big day. No 438 was the first Typhoon squadron to drop 1,000 pound bombs. The Wing remained at Hurn until early April before moving away to Funtington, a very basic Advanced Landing Ground near Thorney Island, where the pilots would undergo dive-bombing training. For the next three months or so Hurn was inundated with Typhoon squadrons, making it the major Typhoon base of the 2nd Tactical Air Force.

The Hawker Typhoon, like the Hurricane, had been designed by Sidney Camm and was developed in 1937 from two prototypes. It had first flown in February 1940, and its subsequent development had been indecently hastened in an attempt to counter the Luftwaffe's new threat,

Hawker Typhoon 1B: Hurn became a major Typhoon base for the 2nd TAF.

the Fw 190, although the 'Tiffy', as it was affectionately called, had to be distinguished with black and white stripes to avoid mistaken identity with the Fw 190. The Typhoon was a large and brutish aircraft, powered by a Napier Sabre 1 piston engine, heavily armed with twelve .303 machine guns (later by four wing-mounted .20mm cannons) and with a speed in excess of 400 mph. It entered the Service in September 1941 with No 56 squadron at Duxford in Cambridgeshire, the same airfield as the Spitfire made its Service entry, and almost immediately some serious problems manifested themselves. There were instances of structural failures around the tail plane, undercarriages had a tendency to collapse, the cockpits leaked carbon monoxide, and furthermore the aircraft's Sabre engine proved to be somewhat temperamental and its rate of climb and performance at high-altitudes were rather disappointing. Slowly all these problems were resolved; the original engine was replaced with the much improved Sabre IIA to C engines, and then the full potential of the Typhoon as a fast low-level strike aircraft was fully realised. In late 1942 it was being trialled in the fighter/bomber role, and known as a 'Bombphoon'. In December 1943 the Typhoons were first armed with eight 60 lb rocket projectiles (RPs), which proved to be their most effective and quite devastating weapons. The Typhoon 1B became a superlative ground attack aircraft, either armed with RPs or bombs (two 500 or 1,000 pound bombs), and the Typhoon squadrons of the 2TAF inflicted merciless destruction on the German ground forces and armour in Normandy and beyond. However, the Typhoon had a relatively short operational life, being quickly replaced after VE-Day by the Hawker Tempest.

On 25th March the Typhoons were joined at Hurn by No 125 (Newfoundland) squadron, a First World War squadron which had been reformed in June 1941 as a night-fighter unit with Beaufighters. It was now equipped with the de Havilland Mosquito NF Mk XVII, the latest night-fighter version of this remarkable and versatile aircraft. The Mark XVIIs were provided with the American SCR720 AI radar, and controlled by 'Starlight' – the Sopley AI radar station to the north of Christchurch. The squadron was commanded by Wing Commander J. G. Topham, DSO, DFC Bar. The squadron's crews made their first claims from Hurn on 24th April when three Junkers 88 were destroyed with another two damaged. At the beginning of May another Mosquito night-fighter squadron, No 604 (County of Middlesex), arrived at Hurn under the command of Wing Commander M. H. Maxwell, DFC. It should be noted that the RAF's night-fighter squadrons were commanded by Wing Commanders, the same as heavy bomber squadrons. Although No 604 was assigned to the 2TAF, it was placed under the operational control of No 11 (Fighter) Group. The squadron had operated from Middle Wallop during the Battle of Britain.

As No 143 Wing left the airfield in early April, it was replaced by another Typhoon Wing, No 124, which also operated under the control of No 83 Group of the 2TAF. Its squadrons, Nos 181, 182 and 247 (China-British), were three of the eleven Typhoon squadrons armed with RPs, the other seven squadrons carried bombs. Indeed it was No 181 squadron that had been instrumental in developing the Typhoon as a fighter/bomber and was the first to be armed with RPs. The Wing would proceed to make concentrated attacks on the French railway system – tracks, tunnels, viaducts and railway stock - as well as targeting coastal defences. By 19th April No 143 Wing had returned to Hurn, where there were now well over 100 Typhoons using the airfield, and in May some 40 Mosquitos were added to the total. This state of affairs posed logistical problems for Group Captain W. E. Surplice, DSO, DFC, the Station Commander, and his hard-pressed ground staff, as they endeavoured to keep all these aircraft serviced, fuelled and armed, let alone accommodating and catering for the large number of airmen that were now stationed at Hurn.

The Typhoon squadrons were in action daily, attacking V1 rocket sites, radar stations along the French coast, defence positions, gun batteries, bridges and road/railway communications, as well as flying 'Roadsteads' (attacks on enemy shipping), fighter sweeps, and armed reconnaissance patrols, known as 'Tactical Rhubarbs'. The strikes against radar stations intensified in the immediate days before the invasion. Flight Lieutenant John Saville of No 439 squadron was killed on 5th June whilst attacking the radar station at Fort George. On the night of 5th/6th June the two Mosquito squadrons were engaged in Operation Outmatch – standing night patrols over the shipping in the English Channel and also over the intended beach-heads.

On D-Day, 88 Typhoon sorties were mounted from Hurn. Gun positions were bombed, followed later in the day by attacks on German troop movements to the south of Caen. Two Typhoons were lost, one piloted by Flying Officer L. R. Allman of No 440 squadron, and the other flown by Flight Sergeant Howard of No 181 squadron, who was flying his first operational sortie; both aircraft were brought down by flak. The following day when 138 sorties were flown, three Typhoons failed to return to Hurn. One of the pilots, Pilot Officer G. Rendle of No 181, baled out near to ships off the Normandy coast but he was dead when picked up. The action increased in momentum over the next few days, with over 150 sorties being flown on the 10th. It was on this day that No 182 squadron, commanded by Major D. H. Barlow of the South African Air Force, occupied B.6 advanced landing strip at Coulombs to the rear of Caen; sadly, Major Barlow would be killed in action later in July. The other two squadrons in the Wing were operating from B.6 strip by 21st June. They were immediately replaced by Nos 183 (Gold Coast), 198, and 609 (West Riding) squadrons of No 123 Wing; the latter squadron returning to Dorset, having flown and served at Warmwell during the Battle of Britain and into 1941. During the next ten days No 123 Wing lost two Typhoons in action – both to enemy flak.

The Canadian Wing, No 143, moved out of Hurn to B.9 strip at Lantheuil on 27th June. These early and rather rudimentary landing strips were virtually within sight of the frontline and there were several instances of Typhoons being destroyed on the ground due to enemy artillery fire! The four squadrons of No 146 Wing of the 84 Group, Nos

193 (Fellowship of the Bellows), 197, 257 (Burma) and 266 (Rhodesia), were the next Typhoon units to use Hurn. They arrived from another Advanced Landing Ground, Needs Ore Point in Hampshire, and would stay for about two weeks. On 13th July a Typhoon from 257 squadron was shot down by Me 109s, and on the following day No 197 lost a Typhoon to Me 109s over Lisieux. It was fairly unusual for Typhoons to fall foul of enemy aircraft, especially Me 109s, most of the Force's Typhoons having been lost to flak. The last Typhoon squadron to use Hurn was No 263, which was also the only Typhoon squadron operating in No 10 Group of the ADGB (Fighter Command); it left Hurn on 23rd July.

During the month there had been a detachment (six) of American Northrop P-61 'Black Widows' based at Hurn. They were the USAAF's first purpose-designed radar-equipped night-fighters. They were very new and, as yet, untried in combat in Europe. The three-man crews were working closely with No 125's crews in order to gain some experience of radar-guided night interceptions. The P-61s operated with the Ninth Air Force's 422nd Fighter Squadron based at Scorton. The crews left Hurn on the 10th without encountering any action. Indeed, on that day Wing Commander G. Maxwell of No 604 squadron accounted for a Junkers 88, which brought his squadron's wartime tally to 100 victories. Four days later the squadron left for Colerne in Wiltshire, though they, too, would later move to the Continent to become the first night-fighters to operate from France.

Another Mosquito squadron, No 418 (City of Edmonton), immediately replaced it. The Canadian crews with their Mosquito FB Mark VIs had been engaged on flying intruder raids over France from Holmsley South in Hampshire. Flight Sergeant Dave McIntosh, a navigator with the squadron, writes in his admirable book, *Terror in the Starboard Seat* that at Hurn, 'there wasn't enough room for everybody so in two weeks we moved again'. Certainly he was right in his assertion that Hurn was crowded, but there was a different reason for his squadron's move – Hurn was about to be handed over to the USAAF. However, before the two Mosquito squadrons left for Middle Wallop on 1st August, they combined for a bombing attack on a massive 'long-range gun' installation at Mimoyecques near Calais. When this site was captured by the Canadian troops in late September it was discovered that the 'guns', or 'Hochdruckepumpe' (high pressure pumps), were

Both Nos 125 and 605 squadrons operated Mosquito night-fighters. This is a NF XII with AI Mk VII radar in the nose. (British Aerospace via B. Micheal)

capable of firing pressurised rocket projectiles towards London at a rate of ten per minute – the so-called V3 secret weapon.

Hurn now became known as Station 492 of the USAAF, and during 4th/5th August the aircraft and the airmen of the Ninth's 397th Bomb Group moved from Rivenhall in Essex, where the Group had been operating since April. It is interesting to note the long arm of coincidence in operation. Group Captain Surplice on leaving Hurn was appointed to RAF Rivenhall. The Group Captain, who had earlier commanded bomber squadrons, was sadly killed in action on 2nd/3rd November when flying a Stirling of No 295 squadron (an original Hurn unit), on a SOE supply mission over Norway.

No 397th Bomb Group was the last B-26 (Marauder) Group to be activated by the Ninth. The Martin B-26 was one of the classic American aircraft of the Second World War; it had sharp clean lines, was very streamlined, with a fuselage that resembled a cigar, and when it first appeared, in November 1940, the American press quickly dubbed it 'the flying torpedo'! The aircraft could carry a bomb load of 4,000 pounds to targets within 500 miles range and at a speed in excess of 260 mph. However, it proved to be a rather difficult aircraft to handle and its high landing and take-off speeds presented problems for inexperienced pilots. As the accident rate rose steadily the aircraft gained a very unfortunate reputation and it became known to its crews as the 'widow maker' or the 'Baltimore whore' (Glenn L. Martin Company was based in Baltimore). It also had a rather unfortunate entry into European

B-26 'Marauder' of 499th Bomb Squadron of 397th Bomb Group. (USAF)

operations with the US Eighth Air Force, as the early bombing missions sustained heavy losses. However, despite this initial grim reputation, which took a considerable time to dispel, the B-26 proved to be one of the most successful medium bombers of the war, with over 5,150 produced, including 520 for the RAF. It never fully attained the renown that its wartime performance justly deserved.

The Group, under the strong leadership of Colonel Richard T. Coiner Jr, had gained a fine reputation as 'Bridge Busters', indeed their last operation from their Essex base on 4th August was to bomb a rail bridge at Épernon, between Chartres and Paris. During their time at Rivenhall the Group had mounted 86 missions for the loss of 16 aircraft. In their relatively brief stay at Hurn the crews notched up another 22 missions, passing their 100th milestone on 17th August. Many of their operations were led by either Colonel Coiner, an ebullient Texan, in his appropriately named aircraft *Lucky Star*, or his deputy, Lieutenant Colonel 'Buster' Dempster, a very experienced pre-war officer. Colonel Coiner would be one of only two Ninth Air Force Commanders to remain in command of the same Group throughout the war. The 397th

145

bombed targets at St Malo, Brest and Rouen, although on the 13th of the month it put up a most creditable performance in blowing up an ammunition train at Corbeil. The Americans left Hurn for A.26 advanced landing strip at Gorges on 30th August, and the Group would later be awarded a Distinguished Unit Citation for destroying a vital bridge in the face of severe flak and fighter opposition during the Battle of the Ardennes.

Hurn was handed back to the RAF on 18th October, but it would not remain very long in the Service. The Ministry of Civil Aviation took over the airfield with effect from 1st November, and it now became the country's main long-haul civil airport. Back in January 1944 BOAC had formed a Development Flight at Hurn, to evaluate new aircraft types and equipment for ultimate post-war use. The Flight had particularly tested an Avro Lancaster Mark 1 for possible airline service, and this aircraft – G-AGJI – became the first 'civilian' Lancaster. The aircraft would undertake a number of proving flights over the next six months and these successful flights led to the conversion of the famous wartime bomber into the Avro 691 Lancastrian – a long-range passenger/freight carrier. In April 1944 a BOAC Avro York had left Hurn on an inaugural service to Morocco and from thence onwards to Cairo.

Lancastrian, G-AGMJ, the type used from March 1945 on the Empire route to Sydney. (Bournemouth International Airport via Mike Phipp)

Bournemouth-Hurn Airport in 1980. (Bournemouth International Airport via Mike Phipp)

The first Lancastrian conversions were undertaken by Victory Aircraft Ltd of Canada, before later being transferred to the parent company, A. V. Roe & Co Ltd. It was on 26th April 1945 that a BOAC Lancastrian – G-AGLF - left Hurn to fly to Australia, the journey lasting 53 flying hours. This successful flight led to the introduction of scheduled services by both BOAC and Qantas which commenced in the following month from Hurn. Already both KLM and Sabena were operating limited services from the airport, and BOAC's Dakotas and Yorks were flying to Europe, Egypt and India. The first survey flight to South

America left Hurn on 9th October with scheduled flights starting at Hurn the following March. The transatlantic service was made by a Douglas DC-4 of American Overseas Airlines in October 1945. Hurn was in the centre of all the pioneering post-war flights, until its thunder was stolen by the opening of Heathrow Airport at the end of May 1946, and Heathrow's recognition as London Airport almost two years later.

Since those heady days Hurn Airport has suffered its share of highs and lows. In April 1969 it was taken over by Bournemouth and Dorset Councils and became known as Bournemouth-Hurn Airport. Hurn is now operated by Bournemouth International Airport Ltd, a member of the National Express Group plc, and the number of passengers using the airport has grown steadily. In 1998 over 300,000 passed through on internal and foreign flights. Also at Hurn is the interesting Jet Heritage Aviation museum, which is located near the passenger terminal, where a number of vintage ex-military jet aircraft are on display; the museum is open every day throughout the year.

6

TARRANT RUSHTON

Tarrant Rushton is perhaps now best remembered as the centre of flying operations for Flight Refuelling Ltd, as it was from 1948 to 1980. But for the last two years of the war it was the home of two transport support squadrons for the Airborne Forces, each involved in the three major airborne operations – Neptune, Market Garden and Varsity. Furthermore it was from this airfield that the giant gliders, the Hamilcars, first went into action. Thus Tarrant Rushton holds a special and unique position in the development and subsequent history of the Airborne Forces.

Construction work on the new airfield was started in September 1942 by George Wimpey & Co Ltd at a site situated between Blandford Forum and Wimborne Minister, about 2½ miles to the east of Blandford and close to the Iron Age hill-fort known as Badbury Rings. Built to a conventional Class A Standard design, it was the only one constructed of this design in Dorset. The airfield was provided with one runway at 2,000 yards and the other two at 1,500 yards each. They formed almost a perfect figure 'A' as can be seen from the illustration. The airfield was originally planned to have five T2 type hangars, though eventually only four were supplied; two along the southern edge of the airfield, one to the north-east and close to the main gate, with a fourth (No 1) on the opposite side of the airfield.

Aerial view of Tarrant Rushton. (Flight Refuelling Ltd via Colin Cruddas)

In mid-May 1943 a RAF advance party arrived to occupy the new airfield, and in the following month Tarrant Rushton was placed under the administrative control of No 10 Group of Fighter Command, though it was planned to house at least one squadron of No 38 Wing, which had been formed to provide air transport support for the fast developing Airborne Forces. Towards the end of the month the first Anti-aircraft Flight, No 4676, arrived to set up the ground defences of the airfield. The Flight was part of the RAF Regiment, which had been officially formed on 1st February 1942 with Major-General Sir Claude Liandet, CBE, DSO, being loaned from the Army to become its first Commandant. The nucleus of the Regiment had been provided by the 'ground gunners', a trade that dated back to 1940 when the responsibility for the defence of RAF airfields was firmly placed with station commanders. The members of the RAF Regiment were dressed in khaki battledress with RAF blue berets and blue 'RAF Regiment' shoulder patches. Their now familiar blue uniform was not introduced until 1950.

The first aircraft to use the airfield, in late September, were Lockheed-Vega Venturas from Sculthorpe in Norfolk, where they had been operating with Nos 21, 464 (RAAF), and 487 (RNZAF) squadrons of No 2 Group of Bomber Command; the squadrons were now re-equipping

Lockheed-Vega Ventura.

with Mosquito FB IVs. The Venturas were twin-engined light patrol bombers originally intended as replacements for Bristol Blenheim IVs. They had been produced by the American company solely for the RAF, and bore a striking resemblance to Hudsons, another Lockheed aircraft operating most successfully with Coastal Command; in fact, its design owed much to this reliable and most useful aircraft. Because of their rather porcine shaped fuselages they were dubbed 'The Flying Pig' or just plain 'The Pig'! Squadron Leader L. H. Trent led his Ventura squadron, No 487 (RNZAF), on a daring low-level raid to Amsterdam power station when ten out of the eleven Venturas were lost, and Squadron Leader Leonard H. Trent, DFC, was three years later awarded the Victoria Cross for 'cool, unflinching courage and devotion to duty in the face of overwhelming odds'. He was then a prisoner of war in the infamous Stalag Luft III. The Venturas were now being allocated to Coastal Command, although these aircraft now residing at Tarrant Rushton would later move to Stoney Cross in Hampshire to equip the new airborne support squadron, No 299, which was in the process of formation. The Venturas would be operated until a sufficient number of Short Stirling IVs became available in the New Year.

The day after the arrival of the Venturas (23rd September) a prototype Albemarle IV landed at Tarrant Rushton with Group Captain W. Cooper,

DFC, of No 38 Wing at the controls. The Albemarle would undertake towing trials with a Horsa glider on behalf of the AFEE (Airborne Forces Experimental Establishment). It was not until the following month that the aircraft most closely associated with wartime Tarrant Rushton – the Handley Page Halifax – arrived there. This famous four-engined heavy bomber, which had first entered the Service in November 1940 with No 35 squadron, became associated with the Airborne Forces eleven months later when a Mark 2 srs 1, R9435, was supplied to the Airborne Forces Development Unit at Ringway near Manchester. The Halifax had been specially modified for the use of paratroopers; a hatch had been cut in the floor with a special winch fitted for the retrieval of the static lines, and later a windscreen was added to protect the paratroopers from being caught up in the aircraft's slipstream. However, it was as glider tugs that the Halifaxes made their name with the Airborne Forces, and in January 1942 they began trials towing Horsa gliders, which became known to the paratroops as 'matchboxes'!

The first Halifaxes to arrive at the airfield came from 'A' Flight of No 295 squadron then at Hurn, and they formed the nucleus of the reformed No 298 squadron, with the necessary crews being transferred from

One of the prototype Hamilcars. (RAF Museum)

152

another support squadron, No 297, based at Stoney Cross. No 298 had originally been formed back in August 1942 but because it saw no action, within two months it had been disbanded. Over the following weeks and months the squadron's crews would be engaged in a number of exercises with Horsa gliders. However, the spacious airfield with its new and sound concrete runways was considered eminently suitable for the use of the large Hamilcar glider, and the squadron also became involved in towing trials with the precious few Hamilcars that were then available.

The G.A.L.49 Hamilcar was the largest and heaviest transport glider used by the Allies during the Second World War. General Aircraft Ltd, which had already produced the very successful G.A.L.48 Hotspur glider, had responded to an Air Ministry specification, X27/40, for a large glider capable of transporting a small tank or armoured vehicles. The original prototype, DP206, first flew on 27th March 1942 at Snaith, towed by a Halifax. The glider had a wingspan of 110 feet, it was 68 feet long and 20 feet high and weighed eight tons unladen. It was almost comparable in dimensions to the Halifax except that it had a six foot larger wing span – a formidable glider in all respects. The Hamilcar's maximum towing speed was 150 mph, but it could dive at 187 mph. The cockpit enclosure for its two pilots was situated high in the upper part of the fuselage to allow the maximum access for its cargo, and it was reached by a ladder mounted from within the fuselage. The glider's maximum load was just under eight tons and it could accommodate a seven ton Tetrach tank or two Universal bren gun carriers. The nose of the fuselage was hinged to facilitate loading and the landing gear was jettisoned in flight, the glider then landing on skis.

Only 20 Hamilcars were built at the Feltham works of General Aircraft Ltd, the remainder were produced in sub-assembly parts by Birmingham Railway Carriage and Wagon Co Ltd, the Co-operative Wholesale Society and AC Motors Ltd. The parts were transported by road, usually to Lyneham, where the glider was assembled and flight tested. Tarrant Rushton would be later used by General Aircraft Ltd as a test centre, at least until the number of aircraft and Horsas housed at the airfield militated against the storage and movement of these large and rather cumbersome gliders, and the testing facilities were moved to Cottesmore. For much of the summer of 1942 the airfields at Chelveston in Northamptonshire and Newmarket Heath in Suffolk were used for towing and load testing trials with the few Hamilcars that had been produced so far. Even by 1st January 1944 there were only 27 Hamilcars built against the hundred that had been ordered, that is in addition to the pre-production trials/training gliders. Ultimately over 400 were built, and in 1944 a powered twin-engined Hamilcar was designed and first flew in February 1945. However, only 22 Mark Xs were produced before VJ Day and they did not see any operational action.

At Christmas 1943 the Army pilots of the 1st Battalion of the Glider Pilot Regiment, which had been formally established in February 1942, were posted to Tarrant Rushton on their return from service in Italy. This was a completely new departure because hitherto the glider pilots had been stationed at either their Regimental Depôt at Tilshead or the Battalion's small airfield at Shrewton whence they would travel to the various RAF airfields, where the transport squadrons were based. For some time Lieutenant-General George J. S. Chatterton, the Commandant of the 1st Battalion, had considered that it would be far better for his glider pilots to be based alongside their RAF colleagues. Chatterton felt the change would improve their close working relationship, joint training could be organised on the stations, and his pilots would have greater opportunity of maintaining their flying skills; they were required to complete a minimum of ten flying hours per month. Chatterton managed to gain the approval of Major-General F. A. M. Browning, the overall Commander of the Airborne Forces, for his proposal and he was a little surprised when the Air Council readily agreed.

The glider pilots were all Army personnel; they had been originally selected for flying training by a joint Army/RAF selection board with the RAF undertaking their flying training. Right from the outset the Army Council had demanded that all glider pilots would be as highly trained and disciplined as infantry troops, so that when the gliders had landed at the assault areas the pilots would be able to make a positive contribution to the battle pending their recovery. Hence why the German Wehrmacht always considered the Glider Pilot Regiment to be an 'elite force'. In April 1942 a brevet displaying blue wings on either side of a crown topped by a lion, was introduced, along with a shoulder patch with a base in Cambridge blue. The Regiment was formally disbanded in 1957, when its last members were transferred into the Army Air Corps.

When the decision was made that the 1st Airborne Division would return to this country after its operations in Sicily and Italy, the Chief of the Air Staff, Air Chief Marshal Sir Charles Portal, agreed that No 38 Wing should be given Group status, which it was in October 1943. Its complement of aircraft was increased to 180 to take account of the increased training commitment, as well as all the preparations for Operation Overlord. In the last week of December the Halifax crews at Tarrant Rushton were engaged in a number of minor exercises with the glider pilots, and the combined training programme continued with a vengeance in the New Year, when three major exercises were mounted, culminating on 14th January with 'Manitoba' working with the men of the 1st Canadian Paratroop Brigade; in this exercise ten Hamilcars were towed, each loaded with a Tetrach tank.

On 7th January Short Stirling IVs of No 196 squadron arrived from Leicester East. This four-engined heavy bomber had entered Bomber Command back in August 1940 and had begun its long operational career in February 1941. Although it appeared somewhat ungainly, it soon gained a reputation of being very sturdy and highly manoeuvrable, and was said to be 'built like a battleship but flew like a bird'. However, by November 1943 Stirlings were beginning to be withdrawn from Bomber Command's main bomber force. Its lower operational ceiling meant that its squadrons suffered proportionally higher losses than Halifax and Lancaster squadrons, and also the bomb bays could not be adapted to carry the larger bombs then being designed. No 196's last operation with Bomber Command had taken place on 10th/11th November 1943 from Witchford in Cambridgeshire, and since that time its crews had been training for the squadron's new role – transport and glider-towing. The Mark IVs had the nose and dorsal turrets removed, there was a large opening in the underside of the rear fuselage for dropping paratroops or agents, and the bomb bay had been adapted for carrying supply containers. The Stirlings would remain at Tarrant Rushton until the middle of March when the squadron left for its D-Day base at Keevil, where it would transport men of the 5th Paratroop Brigade to Normandy.

In late February 1944 'C' Flight of No 298 squadron formed the nucleus of a new Halifax squadron, No 644, under the command of Squadron Leader A. G. Norman; the squadron would serve alongside its sister squadron for the rest of the war. The three squadrons, along with an abundant number of Horsas and the far fewer Hamilcars, meant that the airfield became somewhat crowded. Tarrant Rushton also became a prime venue for high-ranking RAF and Army officers to witness demonstrations of glider techniques and operations. Air Chief Marshal Sir Trafford Leigh-Mallory, the AOC-in C of the Allied Expeditionary Air Forces, visited the airfield in February, and on 22nd April he, along with Air Vice Marshal Hollinghurst, the Group Commander, accompanied General Dwight D. Eisenhower in a review of the two Halifax squadrons and 'C' squadron of the Glider Pilot Regiment. Shortly before D-Day, Field Marshal B. L. Montgomery paid a visit to the airfield to encourage the large number of airborne forces temporarily housed at Tarrant Rushton.

During the first three months of the year the three squadrons were engaged in dropping arms, ammunition and supplies to SOE agents and Resistance fighters in France. In these months leading up to D-Day there was a tremendous and seemingly insatiable demand for such material; over this period some 6,100 supply containers were dropped over France. These operations required the crews to fly at low-level and mainly during the full moon periods in order to locate the dropping zones, which were invariably nothing more than small fields or clearings in woods. The warnings of impending drops were transmitted on the BBC World Service as coded 'personal' messages, one early in the day and then repeated later to confirm that the drop was taking place. In the early days the dropping zones were located by dead reckoning navigation, although by 1944 GEE was being used for navigation and an absolute radio altimeter was essential to determine the correct height for the drop – about 500 feet or less, and at a speed of some 130 mph. The 'S-phone' was used by the reception committee to communicate with the aircraft's crew, as was 'Rebecca'. The supplies were dropped mainly in eight-foot long metal containers, which were designed to later break down into smaller sections to make them more easily transportable. They contained portable radio equipment, specialised tools, money, forged documents, foodstuffs, clothing, compasses, flashlights, batteries, first aid kits and medicines, printing inks and presses, cigarettes, soap, boots, folding bicycles . . . the list of supplies seemed endless. Arms, ammunition, ordinary and plastic explosives, along with detonators, were normally supplied in separate drops.

During May the training exercises with the glider pilots intensified with several being conducted during moonlit nights. As D-Day

A Halifax towing a Horsa.

approached No 298 squadron had over 40 Halifaxes on strength, with
No 644 having 35 ready for operations. There were well over 50 Horsas
at Tarrant Rushton, along with the 'required' 34 Hamilcars and another
eight held in reserve. Six Hamilcars had been lost during training. On
2nd June the airfield was virtually sealed and the aircraft and gliders
painted with their invasion stripes, the gliders with three white bands
on the rear of their fuselages but not on their wings, as was the case with
the aircraft. All the crews and glider pilots were briefed, and they waited
patiently for the order that Operation Neptune – the landing of the
Allied troops by air and sea – was on. The first 'go' signal was received
at 9.00 am on 4th June but this was subsequently cancelled because of
adverse weather in the English Channel. However, in the early hours of
the 5th, the order was given that the invasion would take place the
following day.

Major General Richard 'Windy' Gale of the 6th Airborne Division
planned to use his men like airborne commandos in small parties to take
key specific objectives. Three Albemarle/Horsa combinations left
Tarrant Rushton late on the 5th, they would support the paratroops

157

Famous photograph of Tarrant Rushton on the afternoon of D-Day showing Halifaxes and Horsa/Hamilcar gliders. (Imperial War Museum)

tasked with the capture of an important gun battery at Merville. They were followed by six Halifax/Horsas (three from each squadron) engaged in Operation Deadstick – to capture intact and then secure the bridges over the Caen Canel and the River Orme, which were known to be detonated. The six Horsas had numbers from 91 to 96 chalked on their fuselages, and they carried 181 assault troops of 'D' Company of 2nd Battalion of Oxford & Buckinghamshire Light Infantry (the 'Ox and Bucks') under the command of Major John Howard.

The first Horsa, '91', piloted by Staff Sergeant J. Wallwork, which glided in from 6,000 feet, landed at 00.16 hours on the 6th within 47 yards of the Bénouville bridge (now more famously known as the Pegasus Bridge), probably the first Allied troops to land in Normandy. There was a loss, one glider broke its back on landing trapping and injuring seven men, one fatally. Within 15 minutes the bridge was taken as was the nearby Cafe Gondree (now renamed 'Pegasus Bridge Cafe) – the first building to be liberated in Normandy. This *coup de main* (or sudden vigorous attack) operation was a complete success, although one of the six gliders failed to make the landing zone, it came down several miles to the east beside a bridge over the Dives. Major Howard lost two men dead and five wounded. The six Halifaxes that towed the gliders carried on to bomb an ammunition factory to the south-east of Caen as a diversion.

The code-name for the next phase of the airborne assault was 'Tonga'. In this operation 30 Halifax/Horsas and four Halifax/Hamilcars left Tarrant Rushton in the early hours of D-Day. Two of the Hamilcars failed to arrive at the landing zone due to broken tow-ropes. Eight of the towing aircraft were lost, including a Halifax from No 298 squadron; but the glider pilots suffered higher losses with 34 being killed (17%). The final British part of the airborne assault took place in the evening when 'Operation Mullard' was launched with no less than 248 aircraft and gliders, 32 from the Tarrant Rushton squadrons, with all but two aircraft towing Hamilcars. All of the gliders landed safely at about 21.30 hours near Ranville. One of the Hamilcars was set on fire on the ground by enemy artillery but the Tetrach tank and its driver emerged safely. The squadron lost another Halifax, one of the thirteen aircraft that failed to return.

Almost to the end of the month the two squadrons were engaged in transporting supplies into Normandy as well as recovering Horsa gliders. The Hamilcars were not retrieved, they were considered to be 'write-offs' and only spare parts were removed; it would have been

Two of the Horsa gliders that landed on the banks of the Caen Canal on D-Day. (Imperial War Museum)

quite impossible to tow these heavy gliders from restricted fields. Of the some 230 Horsas taking part in the operations at least 160 were considered capable of repair, although in fact just over 40 were safely brought back. However, the crews did manage to recover a damaged Hurricane, which remained at Tarrant Rushton until it was claimed by its rightful owners.

In July and August the crews returned to their Resistance dropping operations. On 5th/6th July the night was said to be 'clear with a bright moon' and eight crews – four from each squadron - were engaged along with another 21 crews. Sadly a Halifax from No 298 squadron failed to return on this night. During the two months over 530 Resistance sorties were made by the RAF. No 298 lost three Halifaxes in August, one of which, J-LL148, had towed a Hamilcar during Operation Tonga, whereas No 644 lost its first aircraft, T-LL400, to enemy action on 31st August.

In early September two further Allied airborne operations were scheduled. On the first of the month Operation Linnett II – the crossing of the River Meuse – was planned but it was suddenly postponed and two days later cancelled. Then Operation Comet – the crossing of the Rhine in the Wesel area – was prepared for 8th September but this too was postponed for two days, only to be cancelled just five hours before the scheduled take-off time, because the advance of the British XXX Corps had been checked just short of the Dutch frontier. However, 'Comet' was not completely shelved, as it effectively became the blueprint of a greatly enlarged operation, under the code-name 'Market Garden'. It was Field Marshal Montgomery's aim 'to cross the Rhine as quickly as possible . . . by throwing an airborne carpet across the waterways from Eindhoven to Arnhem together with the associated canals'. The reason for the two word code-name was that 'Market' would be the airborne participation engaging the British 1st Airborne Division, the 1st Polish Parachute Brigade, and the American 101st and 82nd Airborne Divisons, with 'Garden' as the British XXX Corps' advance to and beyond Arnhem on the ground. The fame, or infamy, of Market Garden resides in the brutal and costly battle at Arnhem, and this operation has since been described as 'one of the most seriously flawed of all the major operations in World War II'.

The launch of the operation was planned for Sunday 17th September, and it was to be an airborne assault on a quite massive scale. Almost

34,000 Allied airborne troops were involved, 60% by parachute and the rest by gliders, along with 5,000 tons of equipment and some 2,500 armoured vehicles and guns. The first problem was that there was an insufficient number of transport aircraft to carry this large force in one lift, and so it was decided to transport the forces and supplies in three separate air-lifts on consecutive days. According to the grand plan, virtually 90% of the total available glider pilots would be needed for Market Garden, the majority of whom had gained operational experience during the D-Day landings, when the losses of glider pilots had been far fewer than expected.

On 17th September 40 Halifaxes left Tarrant Rushton with 13 Hamilcars and 27 Horsas. The glider pilots came from 'C' squadron of the 2nd Wing of Glider Pilot Regiment, which had its headquarters at Broadwell. The whole formation was airborne within 23 minutes and all units of Nos 38 and 46 Groups were to assemble over Hatfield, and thence fly to Aldeburgh on the Suffolk coast (known as 'Antigua'), and across the North Sea to the Dutch coast at Schouven Island (Bermuda). From there it was about 100 miles (or some 40 minutes flying time) to the dropping and landing zones to the west of Arnhem. The Hamilcars were more prone to crashes, especially when landing on soft ground with their far heavier loads and, unlike the Horsas, they did not have nosewheels; the new 17 pounder anti-tank gun with its towing vehicle was being taken into action by air for the first time. At least four Hamilcars came to grief on landing, one Halifax had returned to Tarrant Rushton with engine trouble, and another lost its glider over England.

On the following day the second air-lift was delayed for about four hours whilst the weather cleared, and 31 Halifax combinations left the airfield and were in the air within 20 minutes. One of the gliders came down in England, and a Hamilcar ditched in the North Sea with just a single artillery officer losing his life. Another Hamilcar came down about 60 miles from the landing zone but fortunately just within the Allies' frontline. From Tuesday until Saturday the RAF's transport aircraft continued to bring in vital supplies, although the two Halifax squadrons would only operate on Tuesday (the 19th), mainly because the Halifaxes were needed to be conserved to tow Hamilcars in any future airborne landings, and also because their carrying capacity was not as great as either the Stirlings or Dakotas. In total 92 sorties had been launched from Tarrant Rushton over the three days, and not a single

Halifax had been lost to enemy action. The RAF lost 64 aircraft in the operation, over 60% of them Stirlings. However, the Glider Pilot Regiment suffered heavy casualties, with over 500 pilots killed or missing in action and another 150 injured. It was as a result of this ill-fated operation that by the end of September the Army reluctantly agreed that RAF pilots (there was now a surplus) be trained as glider pilots to fill the vacancies in the Regiment. The proposal was that the RAF would contribute over 500 glider pilots to the planned target figure of 1,000 by April 1945.

The final major airborne operation of the war – Varsity, the crossing of the Rhine – had been first planned in February 1945 and the operational date was set for 24th March. The mistakes that had been made on Market Garden had been fully assimilated, and the entire air-lift (over 2,000 aircraft and gliders) was planned to be completed within a matter of hours. For this reason the Groups' squadrons were temporarily transferred from their bases in southern England to various airfields in East Anglia. The two RAF Groups would lift the British 6th Airborne Division with the USAAF transporting the US 7th Airborne Division from bases in France.

Nos 298 and 644 squadrons were moved to Woodbridge in Suffolk, the first aircraft and gliders leaving Tarrant Rushton on 15th March. Woodbridge was an Emergency Landing Ground, specially constructed to be used by aircraft landing in distress, and it was known to all aircrews as a 'Prang or Crash-drome'. It had been provided with an immense concrete runway measuring 3,000 yards long by 250 yards wide (five times the width of a normal wartime runway!). Woodbridge proved to be a perfect location for the long take-off distance needed by the Halifax/Hamilcar tows.

From 19th to 24th March Woodbridge was closed to emergency landings whilst the 48 Hamilcars and 12 Horsas were loaded with tanks, jeeps, armoured vehicles, bren gun carriers, ammunition, and in some instances fuel. A RAF officer serving at Woodbridge recalled: 'a large tented accommodation area had been established just back from the main runway towards the eastern end. It reminded me of World War 1 pictures and we wondered what all these Army types, sporting RAF-type wings, were up to . . . all the gliders and tugs were marshalled in orderly lines down at the far end of the runway, the gliders ranged in three rows pointing inwards at 45 degrees. It was all done meticulously, right down to the towing hawsers laid out on the ground from each of the gliders, an impressive sight indeed over the vast Woodbridge runway'.

Then on 24th March at 06.00 hours, on what has been described as 'a bright and sunny morning', the Halifaxes and their tows proceeded to take-off, and within 40 minutes the two squadrons were airborne to join the massive air armada – over 4,600 aircraft and 1,326 gliders. Operation Varsity proved to be a resounding success. Of the 439 combinations that left England, just over 400 reached the assault area, and the RAF lost only four aircraft; 54 of the Halifax combinations from Woodbridge landed successfully. However, once again the Glider Pilot Regiment suffered the heaviest casualties, 173 pilots were killed or missing, with another 77 wounded, or almost a quarter of its strength.

On the squadrons' return to Tarrant Rushton, the crews were once again back on Resistance operations, but this time to Denmark and Norway. On the night of 23rd/24th April a Halifax B VII, NA337, failed to return from a dropping mission over Norway. It had fallen to a Luftwaffe night-fighter, and crashed into Lake Mjosa in Norway. Only the rear tail gunner survived. Some 50 years later the aircraft was brought to the surface, and it is now being restored to its full wartime glory at the RCAF Memorial Museum at Trenton in Ontario.

On VE Day, 8th May, the two squadrons were active landing troops of the 1st Airborne Division at Copenhagen to form an occupation force in Denmark. This was followed shortly by Operation Doomsday, the movement of ground troops and supplies into Norway to assist in the surrender of the German occupation forces in Oslo and other major Norwegian towns. It was in this operation that Air Vice-Marshal J. R. Scarlett-Streatfield, who had been the Commander of No 38 Group since Arnhem, was killed whilst flying as a passenger in a Stirling. In July, No 298 squadron moved out to India with one Flight of Halifaxes, and its sister squadron, No 644, also moved abroad to Palestine in November; although by the end of 1946 both squadrons would have been disbanded. No 644 was reformed as a transport squadron, and renumbered 47, which, at the time of writing, is still operational and stationed at RAF Lyneham.

The airfield was placed under Care and Maintenance status in September 1946, but by the end of the following year the Air Ministry felt it no longer had any use. Just six months later Flight Refuelling Ltd,

Memorial stone at Tarrant Rushton.

the company that Sir Alan Cobham had founded in 1934, leased the airfield from the Air Ministry and moved into Tarrant Rushton. The RAF returned briefly during the early 1950s when No 210 Advanced Flying School was formed there. Flight Refuelling Ltd remained at the airfield until the summer of 1980, and after the company left, contractors moved in to remove the concrete runways and hard standings, with the control tower being demolished in the following year. In June 1982 a memorial plaque, situated close to the former main gate, was dedicated and unveiled, commemorating all the crews and the wartime operations mounted from the airfield.

7

WARMWELL

When the Air Ministry Aerodromes Board selected the 300 acre site about a mile or so to the south of the village of Woodsford for development into a new aerodrome, little did they realise how far-sighted their decision would be. It was planned to be just one of a number of new Armament Practice Camps that would be opened in the late 1930s. However, from the summer of 1940 right through to August 1944 the airfield was an important operational fighter station, used by Spitfires, Hurricanes, Whirlwinds, Typhoons, Thunderbolts and Lightnings, richly rewarding the Air Ministry's relatively small initial investment, as well as its remarkable foresight.

RAF Woodsford, as it was first named, opened in May 1937, and like virtually all pre-war Expansion airfields, it had been provided with grass runways; the main 'run' measured some 1,900 yards positioned north-east to south-west, with a second one slightly shorter at 1,750 yards, and a third at 800 yards. The new aerodrome was bounded to the north by the railway line from Wareham, and situated less than four miles to the south-east of Dorchester. Two months would pass before the first aircraft arrived to form the Station Flight. They were biplanes to tow aerial targets for No 6 Armament Training Camp, which had already settled into the new station.

The new aerodrome owed its existence to the two bombing and gunnery ranges that had been established along the nearby Chesil Beach despite strong local opposition from naturalists and fishermen. No 6

ATC was one of a number of similar camps that opened in the immediate pre-war years, others were at Evanton, Penrhos, Acklington, Jurby and West Freugh, all sited much farther north than Woodsford. These Practice Camps were intentionally not built to the elaborate and somewhat luxurious standards of most permanent Expansion stations, they were solely approved as hutted camps, intended for purely temporary occupation by the various squadrons using the ranges.

In April 1938 the Camp became known as No 6 Armament Training School, and was under the control of No 25 Group of Training Command. The School was equipped with a rare mixture of aircraft, most of which had been removed from frontline squadrons and relegated to training duties. They included Handley Page Harrows, Hawker Hind biplanes, Boulton and Paul Sidestrands and Overstrands, the latter being the first to have a totally enclosed power-operated gun turret. The only aircraft amongst the motley assortment with any claim to modernity were Hawker Henley IIIs. They had been designed as light bombers but because of their rather inadequate performance few were produced, and they entered the Service with Bombing and Gunnery Schools as 'high-speed target tows', capable of a maximum towing speed of 270 mph. All these aircraft would display broad black diagonal bars to identify them as towers of the bright yellow drogue sleeves.

The Air Ministry decided in July 1938 to rename the station Warmwell, derived from the small village about a mile and a half to the south. The reason for this change was to avoid any confusion with Woodford in Cheshire, an airfield attached to A. V. Roe & Co Ltd's aircraft factory. Indeed, it was this company's most successful Service aircraft – Avro 652A Anson – that became a frequent visitor to Warmwell in the early days.

The Anson, familiarly known as 'The Faithful Annie', was probably one of the best loved aircraft in the RAF because so many crews had been trained in them. It was the first monoplane to enter the RAF, and also was the first to employ a retractable undercarriage. The aircraft had originally been developed as a small passenger carrier for Imperial Airways, hence the array of windows along the fuselage, which gained it the nickname 'The Flying Greenhouse'! The Anson entered the Service in March 1936 basically as a navigational and general aircrew trainer but it also served as a coastal reconnaissance aircraft with Coastal Command, which at the outbreak of war had eleven Anson squadrons.

166

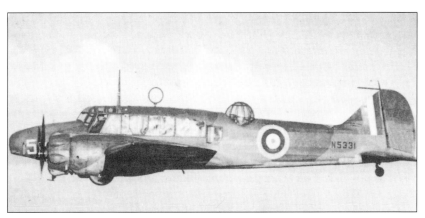

'The Faithful Annie' – Avro Anson.

On 5th September 1939 it was an Anson that became the first RAF aircraft to attack a German U-boat. Ansons would remain on active service with Coastal Command until January 1942 when they were replaced by Lockheed Hudsons. Over 20,000 Ansons (of various Marks) were built, making it one of the longest production runs of any British aircraft, and they were not finally retired until June 1968 – over 30 years of 'faithful' service.

Ansons of Nos 206 and 220 squadrons were the first to arrive at Warmwell and were engaged on coastal patrol exercises. But in the autumn of 1938 No 217 (Exeter) squadron brought its Ansons from Boscombe Down, where the squadron had been re-formed in March 1937. Like all RAF squadrons it had its own identification code, normally comprising two letters, which, along with the aircraft's individual letter, were boldly displayed on the fuselage either side of the RAF roundel. In most cases, but not all, the pre-war codes were comprehensively changed with the advent of war; thus 217's Ansons originally carried 'YQ' but these were altered to 'MW'. The squadron would remain at Warmwell undertaking coastal patrols until 2nd October 1939 when it moved away to Cornwall to open up the new airfield at St Eval.

On 2nd September 1939 No 10 Air Observation School was formed from the existing Training School. It should be noted that only in early 1938 had the Air Ministry begun recruiting personnel specially to be trained as Observers. Then, on 1st November, the School was redesignated No 10 Bombing and Gunnery School and five days later the Central Gunnery School (CGS) was formed with a mix of bombers for training purposes varying from the light Fairey Battles to the far heavier Whitleys, Wellingtons and Hampdens. The CGS provided a three week course training gunnery instructors, and first was mounted on the 13th of the month. The School would remain at Warmwell until June 1941, even though the airfield was a very active fighter operational station. When the CGS settled into its final wartime station at Sutton Bridge in Lincolnshire it gained a reputation as a 'centre of excellence', mainly under the command of Wing Commander A. G. 'Sailor' Malan, DSO Bar, DFC Bar, of Battle of Britain fame.

The fall of France in June 1940 certainly made the west of England far more vulnerable to Luftwaffe attacks from airfields just across the Channel, and fighter airfields in the area were at a premium. Warmwell was in a prime position to provide valuable fighter cover for the shipping convoys passing along the English Channel as well as affording protection to the nearby important Naval base at Portland. The airfield was therefore transferred into No 11 Group of Fighter Command to operate as a satellite for Sector 'Y' airfield at Middle Wallop, although it would become operational under the newly formed No 10 Group.

The first fighters to use Warmwell were the incomparable Spitfire Is of No 609 (West Riding) squadron, which had been transferred into Middle Wallop on 4th July from Northolt in order to bolster the meagre resources of the new Group. The squadron had been formed in Yeadon in February 1936 and was one of a number of Auxiliary Air Force squadrons that made such an important contribution to the RAF throughout the war. The squadron's badge incorporated a white rose to show its Yorkshire origins, with its motto 'Tally Ho' most appropriate for a fighter squadron! The squadron was now commanded by Squadron Leader H. S. 'George' Darley, a regular officer, who was described by his pilots as the 'little dynamo'. Whilst operating over the Dunkirk beaches at the end of May the squadron had fought valiantly, losing five pilots including a Flight Commander.

For almost the next 18 months it would be Spitfires that would grace the airfield; indeed 'grace' is an appropriate word to describe these aircraft, even today the sight and sound of a Spitfire performing at an air

Spitfire I, P9322, flown by Pilot Officer D. M. Crook, DFC, of No 609 squadron. (Imperial War Museum)

display can still generate considerable admiration and excitement for its truly classic lines and performance. This remarkable fighter had originated from an Air Ministry Specification F7/30 (later F37/34) to which R. J. Mitchell, the chief designer of Supermarine Aviation, responded with his first design of a revolutionary monoplane, the F400. His company had gained a fine reputation with seaplanes, and the Spitfire was a derivative of the splendid S6B, which won the Schneider Trophy in 1931. But it was the successful marriage of Mitchell's airframe with a Rolls-Royce PV12 engine, later named 'Merlin', that ensured the aircraft's quite astounding success. The first prototype (K5054) flew on 6th March 1936, and was already known as a 'Spitfire', though Mitchell was not particularly impressed with the name. He is reported to have said, 'Sort of bloody silly name they *would* choose'! Sadly Mitchell did not live long enough to witness his aircraft's great success, he died in June 1937. The first Spitfires entered the Service with No 19 squadron at Duxford in Cambridgeshire on 4th August 1938, and it could be said that from then the aircraft never looked back.

The Spitfire I had a top speed of 360 mph at 18,500 feet with a fine rate of climb, and was thought to be the fastest fighter in the world. Armed with eight .303 Browning machine guns, it was a formidable fighting machine, as many Luftwaffe pilots later testified. A total of over 1,560 Mark 1s were built, including about 50 by Westland Aircraft Ltd. However, over 20,000 Spitfires were finally produced in a bewildering array of Marks, and their last operational sorties were flown in June 1954. Most of the famous wartime fighter pilots flew Spitfires at some time or other. 'Sailor' Malan was most impressed, '[She] had style and was an obvious killer . . . moreover she was a perfect lady. She had no vices. She was beautifully positive'. Douglas Bader considered it, 'the aeroplane of one's dreams.'

No 609's pilots quickly became inured to a regular routine – one day on 15 minutes readiness at Middle Wallop, followed by a day of rest, and then a day of readiness at Warmwell, where the squadron maintained a servicing flight. They found that the amenities at Warmwell were rather basic, as the best and most comfortable accommodation was occupied by the airmen serving in the CGS. They invariably used tented accommodation at their dispersal area on the northern side of the airfield. Mostly the pilots arrived at first light from Middle Wallop and returned to the relative comfort of their permanent station during the late evening.

The airfield was used by the squadron on 6th July but the pilots had to wait another three days before they encountered any real action. Pilot Officer D. M. Crook accounted for a Junkers 87 Stuka over Portland, but sadly Flying Officer Drummond-Hay was lost over the sea. Crook would be awarded the DFC in October, but like so many Battle of Britain pilots failed to survive the war. Two days later, on the 11th, whilst protecting a convoy in Lyme Bay two pilots were lost, both of whom had been ex-Auxiliary Air Force airmen. Then on the 13th the squadron claimed two Me 110s over Portland Bill. One fell to Flying Officer John C. Dundas, who added to his total seven days later, and he would become the squadron's most successful pilot in the weeks and months ahead. However, by the end of July another pilot failed to return, Pilot Officer J. R. Buchanan, RAFVR, who had shared in the squadron's first wartime victory back in February, when operating from Drem in Scotland.

No 10 Bombing and Gunnery School was moved out of the frontline to Dumfries in Scotland, and its place was taken by a Spitfire squadron, No 152 (Hyderabad), which had been moved down from Acklington in Northumberland. The squadron had originally been formed in 1918 as

Fighter pilots relax at Warmwell. (Imperial War Museum)

the second night-fighter squadron, but like so many squadrons it had been disbanded in 1919. Re-formed in October 1939 with Gloster Gladiator biplanes, it was now commanded by Squadron Leader Peter K. Devitt, another Auxiliary Air Force airman, following the loss of the first Squadron Commander in February. The squadron's pilots had first seen action in January and in the following month they had claimed their first victories – two Heinkel 111s; in fact by coincidence on the 27th of that month both 152 and 609 each claimed a He 111. One brief history of No 152 squadron comments: '[the squadron] flew from Warmwell covering the Channel, South Coast and were drawn into the London

171

battles although it was really too far to make a full contribution to these'. This seems rather scant regard for the squadron's efforts in the Battle of Britain when it lost 14 pilots, one of the highest casualty rates for a Spitfire squadron.

In comparing the two Spitfire squadrons, it can be said that No 152 was a more representative Battle of Britain squadron with a fairly even balance of pre-war and Volunteer Reserve pilots, of which about one third were Sergeants (the average for Fighter Command). About 14% of the pilots hailed from either Commonwealth or European countries, again about the norm for the Command, as indeed was the average age of its pilots – 23 years. On the other hand No 609 was almost exclusively manned by officer pilots, only two Sergeants flew with it during the Battle of Britain. Because most of the pilots were either AAF or VR airmen they were therefore older with an average age of 26+ years, which was rather high for a fighter squadron. No 609, rather unusually, had three of the seven American pilots 'officially' known to have flown in the Battle of Britain; it was thought that more Americans fought in the Battle, having volunteered in Canada.

On 20th July, just one day after flying its first operational sorties from Warmwell, No 152 squadron suffered its first loss when Pilot Officer F. H. Posener went down off the Isle of Wight; he was one of 21 South African airmen that flew in the Battle. Five days later the squadron opened its Battle of Britain score with a Dornier and Junkers 87 being claimed by Pilot Officer Ralph 'Bob' Wolton, a pre-war officer, who shared the Dornier with Flying Officer E. C. 'Jumbo' Deanesley. Deanesley was shot down but picked up from the sea by a merchant vessel in Lyme Bay, and on 30th September he would again suffer the same fate, this time rescued by the ASR services; Deanesley would survive both the Battle and the war, ending up as a Wing Commander.

There was an almost ominous lull in Luftwaffe activity in the area until the first week of August, in fact Flying Officer John Dundas later recalled that 'for 609 the Nazi blitz began on 8th August'.This was the day that Convoy CW9, code-named 'Peewit', was virtually decimated by Junkers 87s on its passage westwards through the English Channel. On this day No 609 claimed three Me 109s and two Ju 87s destroyed without loss. Three days later (the 11th) No 152 lost another pilot, Pilot Officer J. S. B. Jones, who had baled out but was found to be dead on recovery, but the pilots of the two squadrons managed to account for six enemy aircraft. The following day two pilots from No 152 failed to return to Warmwell. One of them, Pilot Officer Douglas C. Shepley, would be remembered by the 'Shepley Spitfire', which was purchased by his family and friends; it is also the name of a public house in Totley near Sheffield, South Yorkshire, where the Shepley family were local landowners. Shepley's brother, a Lysander pilot, had been killed earlier in May.

On 13th August, the Luftwaffe's 'Adler Tag' or 'Eagle Day', No 609's pilots claimed twelve aircraft, ten of them Junkers 87s, without losing a pilot. No 152 managed to bag another Stuka, which fell to Flight Lieutenant Derek Boitel-Gill (or 'Bottled Gull'), who had been a pilot with Imperial Airways before joining the pre-war RAF. He would claim five victories in one week during August and was awarded the DFC in October. In the following month Boitel-Gill was given the command of the squadron, but was unfortunately killed in a flying accident (as a Wing Commander) in August 1941. It was a sad fact of operational flying and service that over one quarter of those pilots who managed to survive the Battle of Britain would be killed later in the war.

Two days later, according to the *Official History of the RAF*, 'Fierce battles developed near Portsmouth and Portland'. Both squadrons survived a day of intense and concentrated aerial combat without loss and they claimed ten victories in total. On what has now become known as the 'Hardest Day' (Sunday 18th) over 100 Ju 87s, strongly supported by Me 109s, attacked Poling Radar station, and the airfields at Ford, Thorney Island and Gosport during the early afternoon. No 152's Spitfires countered their withdrawal across the Isle of Wight, and they claimed eight Ju 87s along with a Me 109. The Stukas were so badly mauled, with over one third either shot down or severely damaged, that they withdrew from the Battle. One of the squadron's young pilots, Pilot Officer Eric S. Marrs, a 19 year old known as 'Boy', achieved his first confirmed victory. Marrs was probably the epitome of the public's image of a Battle of Britain pilot – young, an ex-public schoolboy and a graduate of RAF Cranwell College. He would be awarded the DFC in December but sadly he was killed whilst on a light bomber escort mission to Brest in July 1941, and is buried in France.

Warmwell first attracted the Luftwaffe's attention on 25th August when some 20 bombs struck the station sick quarters and hangars, as well as leaving several craters around the airfield and a number of unexploded bombs, which took a few days to clear. Fortunately there were no casualties. As London and the South-East, along with the fighter airfields in No 11 Group, became increasingly the targets for the Luftwaffe during the first two weeks of September, No 609 squadron was frequently called upon to assist No 11 Group's hard pressed squadrons. On the 7th of the month its pilots claimed six enemy aircraft including two Dornier 17 bombers (the 'Flying Pencils'), and on 'Battle of Britain Day' (the 15th) another five 'Flying Pencils' fell to their guns, although one pilot, Pilot Officer G. N. Gaunt, was shot down by a Me 110 and crashed in Kent. On the same day six pilots of No 152 were in action over Portland attacking a force of Heinkel 111s, two of which were destroyed.

However, it was during the last week of the month that both squadrons were under considerable pressure, which culminated in the heavy daylight raid directed at Bristol and Yeovil, but when Sherborne suffered so grievously. The Luftwaffe lost 19 aircraft on this operation with at least another 16 damaged, of which three were claimed by the two squadrons. No 152 lost Sergeant L. A. E. Reddington, who was shot down over the sea, the sixth fatality for the squadron in the month. During September the two squadrons had managed to claim over 50 enemy aircraft destroyed in total, with No 609 losing just two pilots. Pilot Officer R. F. G. Miller collided with a Me 110 over Cheselbourne on the 27th of the month.

On 4th October No 609 squadron had a new Commanding Officer, Squadron Leader M. Lister Robinson, DFC, who had previously led No 238 squadron; 'George' Darley had been promoted and left to become the Station Commander at Exeter. He would survive the war and retired from the RAF in 1959 as a Group Captain. On the afternoon of the 7th when Yeovil was heavily raided, the two squadrons accounted for nine enemy aircraft, but in the process each lost a pilot. Pilot Officer H. J. Akroyd of No 152 was badly burned and died the following day. Sergeant Feary's Spitfire was badly damaged in combat with a Me 109 and he tried to make it back to Warmwell; however, he was forced to bale out, unfortunately at too low a height and he was killed. Feary, who had served in the RAFVR since 1936, was a native of Derby, and in July 1987 a permanent memorial to him was opened in the Derby Industrial Museum. On the 21st of the month No 609 passed an important milestone when Flight Lieutenant Howell and Pilot Officer Hill recorded its 100th victory – a Junkers 88.

For the majority of November there was little action of note, at least until the 28th when both squadrons suffered losses. Flight Lieutenant John C. Dundas, DFC, 609's most successful pilot with 11½ victories to his name, managed to bring down Major Helmut Wick, the Kommodore of the prestigious JG2 (Jagdgeschwader) and a leading Luftwaffe ace with 56 credited victories. Shortly after destroying Wick's Me 109, Dundas was shot down by the Major's wingman. Another of 609's Spitfires had already fallen to Major Wick. Pilot Officer A. R. Watson, an ex-Cranwell graduate, who had survived all the earlier fighting, also failed to return. Dundas' younger brother, Hugh or 'Cocky', became the youngest Group Captain at the age of 23 years, and survived the war with a DSO Bar, DFC Bar as one of the famous wartime fighter pilots. The Dundas brothers, like the Buftons, were just one of a number of RAF families that served with such distinction, amongst the others being the Atcherleys, the Cheshires and the MacRoberts.

From the end of November No 609 moved into Warmwell and operated from there until 24th February 1941, when it was immediately replaced by another Spitfire squadron, No 234 (Madras Presidency), which had been the highest scoring squadron in No 10 Group during the Battle of Britain. It was commanded by Squadron Leader M. V. 'Mindy' Blake, DFC, a New Zealander who had joined the RAF in 1937. The two Warmwell squadrons would now be mainly engaged on convoy patrols and bomber escorts.

On 1st April 1941 the airfield was bombed by three Heinkel 111s making a surprise low-level raid. Several workshops were damaged, and ten airmen were killed including Sergeant Fawcett, one of No 152's pilots. As a result of this raid all the aircrew were dispersed away from the station at night. The Luftwaffe returned on 11th May but little damage was sustained. By that time No 152 squadron had left for Portreath in Cornwall, being briefly replaced by No 118 squadron. There was a further change in June when the CGS moved out to West Freugh in Northern Ireland and Warmwell became a purely fighter station.

During early July, No 234 squadron was re-equipped with Mark II Spitfires, which had been provided with a single drop tank sited in the middle part of the left wing to increase their operational range. On 10th July the squadron was engaged on escorting 24 Blenheims making coastal sweeps from Le Havre to Cherbourg. One Blenheim was lost along with two Spitfires. Piloted by Wing Commander Blake, DFC, the Blenheim had ditched in the sea after a fierce combat with Me 109s during which Blake claimed to have destroyed two. It was reported that the Wing Commander paddled his dinghy for about twelve hours before being rescued. This was an early successful use of the 'K' type dinghy, recently issued to fighter pilots. Previously their only life support had been the so-called 'Mae West' life jacket. Just 15 days later another of the squadron's pilots, Sergeant R. C. Hoornaart, ditched in the sea about three miles from Exmouth and was successfully rescued.

By the autumn the squadron began to be supplied with Mark V Spitfires, which were powered with Merlin 45 engines, giving the aircraft a maximum speed of about 375 mph at 13,000 feet. This Mark became the mainstay of Fighter Command for the next twelve months or so, with almost 6,500 being produced, although the aircraft ultimately proved to be inferior in performance to the Luftwaffe's new fighter – the Focke-Wulf 190.

However, the airfield was about to move into a more offensive operational role, with the arrival, in September, of Hurricane IIbs or 'Hurribombers' of a Polish squadron – No 302 – which had adopted the regional title 'Poznan' from their homeland, and had served during the Battle of Britain. This famous fighter had been designed by Sidney Camm, the chief designer of Hawker Aircraft Ltd, as a development of his successful Fury biplane. It first flew in November 1935, and entered the Service in December 1937. The Hurricane squadrons were the backbone of Fighter Command during 1939 and 1940, destroying more enemy aircraft during the Battle of Britain than all other defences both land and air combined. The 'Hurry' was fondly admired and trusted by all who flew the aircraft, inspiring in its pilots an immense and deep loyalty. Without doubt the Hurricane was an outstanding combat aircraft, now beginning to enter a new role as a fighter/bomber. The Mark IIb was powered by a Rolls-Royce Merlin XX engine with a low-speed supercharger, it was armed with twelve .303 machine guns and capable of carrying two 250 or 500 pound bombs.

The squadron's pilots would be mainly engaged in making ground offensive sweeps over Normandy and Brittany, and they stayed at Warmwell for about five weeks. On 5th November No 234's Spitfires left for Ibsley in Hampshire, and were immediately replaced with the Hurricane IIbs of a Canadian squadron – No 402 (Winnipeg Bear). The Canadians had been working up to operational readiness with its

WARMWELL

Hurricane of No 402 squadron being loaded with two 250 pound bombs.

'Hurribombers' from Rochford in Essex; indeed on 1st November eight pilots had bombed Berck-sur-Mer airfield in France. No 402 was commanded by Squadron Leader V. B. Corbett, a Canadian Battle of Britain pilot, who had been shot down in flames on 31st August 1940 whilst flying with No 1 (RCAF) squadron. He suffered burns and had not long returned to operational flying. The Canadians would remain at Warmwell until March 1942 when the squadron moved farther inland to Colerne in Wiltshire.

In November 1941, No 10 Group established a 'Practice Camp' at Warmwell for its fighter squadrons to use the two firing ranges at the Chesil Beach. For this reason No 1487 Target Towing Flight was formed during the month equipped with the much loved 'Lizzies' or Westland Lysanders, which had now been taken off operations, except, of course, for landing and picking-up agents in occupied France. Later in the month some additional Lysanders arrived; they were attached to No 276 (Air/Sea/Rescue) squadron, which hitherto had been operating from Harrowbeer in Devon. The Lysanders were employed to spot ditched crews and pilots, whilst the Walrus did the actual rescue. The squadron also had a number of Ansons and Spitfire (ASR) IIs, which carried 'E' type survival packs.

By mid-1941 the chances of a successful rescue of airmen from the sea had risen to about 35%, and in August Coastal Command had been

Supermarine Walrus on A/S/R practice landing. (via T. Woods)

given the responsibility of A/S/R. Until then it had rested with Fighter Command, really since the Battle of Britain when it had been started as a rather hastily improvised service. The Command's existing A/S/R units were all upgraded to squadron strength and their operational limit had been extended from 20 to 40 miles. By the end of the war a total of over 3,723 RAF and 1,998 American airmen (as well as many Luftwaffe airmen) had been rescued from the waters around Britain by the various A/S/R services, fully justifying the Service's motto; 'The sea shall not have them'. Two other A/S/R squadrons, Nos 275 and 277, would also operate from Warmwell during 1943/4.

On 3rd March 1942 a new squadron was formed at Warmwell, No 175, under the command of Squadron Leader F. M. Smith and would be equipped with Hurricane IIbs. The pilots spent about five weeks in preparations for their first operational sorties, and their first bombing mission was mounted on 16th April to Maupertas airfield. Two enemy minesweepers were sunk during May, but perhaps their most notable operation from Warmwell was the ill-fated Operation Jubilee – the raid on Dieppe on 19th August. The squadron was now commanded by Squadron Leader John R. Pennington-Legh, DFC, a former torpedo bomber pilot. Only two of the eight Hurricane squadrons taking part

178

were flying 'Hurribombers'. At 4.40 am on the 18th he led out nine Hurricanes, the squadron's first mission of the day, to attack the 'Göring' heavy gun battery just inland from Dieppe; each of the Hurricanes was carrying two 500 pound bombs, and would dive from 3,000 to 800 feet on their bombing run. The second mission left the airfield just after 10 am, led by Pilot Officer R. A. Peters, DFC, (RNZAF) to the 'Rommel' four gun positions sited to the east of Dieppe, and although the pilots encountered heavy flak all returned safely. The third and final mission was directed against the 'Hindenburg' coastal batteries. No 175 lost one aircraft, but its pilot, Pilot Officer D. I. Stevenson, baled out unhurt, and besides their accurate bombing the squadron claimed a Heinkel 111 and Fw 190 destroyed, with another damaged. Squadron Leader Pennington-Legh was awarded a Bar to his DFC, and Flight Lieutenant D. Murchie (RCAF) a DFC. Wing Commander 'Mindy' Blake, who was flying as a 'guest' with No 130 squadron, was shot down and taken prisoner-of-war.

About a week later the squadron was joined at Warmwell by another 'Hurribomber' unit, No 174, which had also taken part in the Dieppe raid, but had suffered the loss of five pilots (including their squadron commander). It was now commanded by Squadron Leader William W. McConnell, DFC Bar, who had also been in action over Dieppe. However, the 'Hurribomber' was now considered a little too vulnerable for ground attack operations, and it would be replaced by the Hawker Typhoon, which had received its baptism of fire in this role at Dieppe. The first Typhoon Wing, which had been formed at Duxford, had been in action over Dieppe, and one of its squadrons, No 56, had been commanded by Squadron Leader Hugh Dundas, DFC.

On 21st September No 266 (Rhodesian) squadron, the precursor of a number of Typhoon squadrons, arrived from Duxford when the Duxford Typhoon Wing was broken up. It had been the second squadron to be equipped with Typhoons, and was commanded by an experienced Rhodesian airman, Squadron Leader Charles L. Green, DFC. The pilots undertook regular patrols along the south coast as a counter to the Luftwaffe's low-level 'tip and run' raids made by Fw 190s against coastal towns and targets that were causing so much annoyance and damage; they were officially known as 'anti-Rhubarb patrols'. At this time the Typhoon was the only RAF fighter capable of matching the Fw 190 in speed. No 266 would stay at Warmwell until early January

1943, although it was detached to Predannack in Cornwall during November.

During the winter of 1942/3 the bombing range at Chesil Beach was used to test the feasibility of Barnes Wallis' theory of a 'bouncing bomb' or 'Spherical bomb', which was ultimately used so successfully by No 617 (Dambusters) squadron in May 1943. A Wellington – BJ985/G – from Vickers-Armstrong's airfield at Weybridge in Surrey made the first drops of the practice bombs – smooth wooden spheres code-named 'Upkeep' – in early December, followed by another trial later in the month, neither particularly successful. With the Wellington using Warmwell as a forward base another two trials were conducted on 9th and 10th January, followed later in the month by two further tests. The most promising trial was completed on 5th February when a 3' 10" diameter smooth wooden ball revolving at some 450 rpm achieved a range of 1,315 yards, almost twice the expected distance. Before the project team moved to Reculver Bay off the Kent coast, the final two trials were completed at Chesil Beach on 8th and 9th March. Eleven days later 'Squadron X' was formed under the command of Wing Commander Guy Gibson, DSO, Bar, DFC, which a week later became officially known as No 617 squadron and the Reculver trials commenced in mid-April.

Whilst this highly secret experimental work was being undertaken off the Chesil Beach, the Typhoons and Whirlwinds continued to use Warmwell for their operations. The latter aircraft was certainly one of the rarer fighters to see service with the RAF, only two squadrons, Nos 137 and 263 (Fellowship of the Bellows), being equipped with them. No 263 had arrived at Warmwell in September with their twin-engined fighters, which were not newcomers to the airfield, having made brief appearances during June and December 1941. The Westland Whirlwind was the first twin-engined fighter to enter the Service in July 1940. It was uniquely armed with four 20 mm cannons mounted in the nose, which at the time was quite formidable firepower. However, the aircraft was continually plagued with niggling problems from its small Rolls-Royce Peregrine engines, making servicing and maintenance most difficult and preventing the full development and potential that it merited. The Whirlwind had an excellent performance at low-level with a far superior operational range than most fighters, so it was considered ideal for bomber escort duties, though it would find its true métier as a

Westland Whirlwind: No 263 squadron was one of only two squadrons to be equipped with this fighter.

fighter/bomber able to carry up to 1,000 pounds of bombs. Just 114 of the aircraft were built, the last one coming off the production lines at Yeovil in January 1942.

The squadron was commanded by Squadron Leader R. S. Woodford, DFC, an ex-Battle of Britain pilot, who was posted missing in December 1942. It would operate from Warmwell until early December 1943 with brief periods of detachment away from the airfield. The pilots were mainly engaged on escort duties but during the summer of 1943 they became increasingly involved in offensive sweeps and 'Roadsteads'; in August they managed to destroy five E-boats as well as sink an armed trawler. Their final operation with Whirlwinds was mounted on 24th October to the port of Cherbourg, when two aircraft failed to return. Another two were 'written-off' due to battle damage, but this was of little concern as the squadron was already beginning to re-equip with Typhoons.

For much of 1943 the Whirlwinds shared the airfield with the Typhoons of No 257 (Burma) squadron, better known as the 'Death or Glory Boys' from their squadron's motto. The squadron had converted to Typhoons in July 1942 and became operational with them at Exeter before moving to Warmwell in early January. Initially there were several servicing problems with the aircraft as the Napier Sabre engines could

Hawker Typhoon 1B of No 257 squadron at Warmwell, May 1943. (via J. Adams)

be rather temperamental at times, nevertheless the pilots flew bomber escort sorties, as well as acting as escorts to Typhoon bombers. By July they were also flying 'Roadsteads' and offensive sweeps. The squadron left Warmwell for about a month, and when they returned in mid-September, the pilots began practice bombing. At the end of the year No 257, commanded now by Squadron Leader Ronald H. Fokes, DFC, DFM, was one of 20 Typhoon squadrons preparing for their role in the 2nd Tactical Air Force. However, they spent most of their time flying coastal patrols in a defensive role, as well as undertaking long-range escorts for the USAAF's B-17s. It was not until 4th January 1944 that they went out on their first bombing mission when a V1 rocket site was the target, but within two weeks the squadron had left for Beaulieu and would ultimately operate under No 146 Wing of 2TAF from Needs Ore Point in Hampshire.

Briefly during the summer of 1943 another Mark of Hurricanes operated from Warmwell – IVs – which were highly specialised ground attack aircraft. They had the more powerful Merlin 24 or 27 engines and had been built with the so-called 'Universal wing', which could accommodate a variety of armament and weapons – machine guns, two Vickers S anti-tank guns, bombs, smoke curtain canisters, drop tanks or up to eight rocket projectiles. Such a varied selection of weapons extended the operational life of the doughty Hurricane until 1947. Without doubt the Hurricane was one of the most outstanding combat aircraft to serve in the RAF with more than 14,000 being ultimately produced.

These Hurricane IVs were operated by No 164 (Argentine-British), commanded by Squadron Leader D. P. McKeown, DFC, and had arrived from Middle Wallop in late June. Although the squadron only stayed for about six weeks, the pilots were quickly into fighter sweeps over Northern France, as well as patrolling the English Channel seeking out likely targets. It was not until the squadron had left Warmwell in early August that the pilots made their rocket projectile attack, although like most other squadrons No 164 would be equipped with Typhoons prior to D-Day.

Although Warmwell had been allocated to the USAAF as a fighter base back in August 1942, the Eighth Air Force had not taken up the option mainly because of the airfield's distance away from its heavy bomber bases in East Anglia. On a few occasions Warmwell had been used as a forward landing airfield for the Eighth's fighters when its bombers were attacking targets in Northern France, most recently on 22nd September 1943 when some 60 P-47s of the 4th Fighter Group arrived en route to Vannes airfield. However, in March 1944 Warmwell was handed over to the USAAF's Ninth Air Force, and it became known as 'Station 454'. The airmen of the 474th Fighter Group arrived on 12th March. They decamped at the nearby Moreton railway station, and as a result often referred to their base as 'Moreton'. They found that a Typhoon squadron, No 263, was occupying the airfield; these 'old' Warmwell residents had arrived on 6th March and would remain until the 19th. The squadron decided to put on a welcoming air display for their American comrades on the 15th, but sadly one of the Typhoons spun out of control when the pilot was completing a low roll and the aircraft crashed about a half a mile from Warmwell; the pilot, a namesake of this author, Pilot Officer Graham Smith, was killed.

The Group's three squadrons – 428th to 430th – were equipped with Lockheed P-38s (Lightnings), just one of three Groups in the Ninth to operate this twin-engined fighter. The P-38 was a brilliant aircraft in concept and at the time of its design (1937) it was far in advance of contemporary fighters. This large twin-boom and twin-engined aircraft

P-38 'Lightning' coming in to land. (National Archives & Records Administration)

entered the US Army Air Corps in 1941, and perhaps its major attraction was its operational range – the first P-38s to arrive in this country were flown across the Atlantic. The fighter was, quite rightly, seen to be the answer to the Eighth Air Force's heavy bomber losses. However, its Allison engines proved to be somewhat unreliable in the cold and damp Northern European climate, especially at high altitudes, and the cockpit heating was always less than satisfactory, making combat flying decidedly uncomfortable for its pilots. Without doubt the aircraft was fast, about 410 mph at 25,000 feet, and armed with four .50 machine guns plus two 20 mm cannons grouped together in the nose, it was a really formidable fighter. The Eighth Air Force had developed the aircraft's potential as a fighter/bomber, able to carry two 1,000 pound bombs, and, certainly by 1944, the P-38 had become a more than effective low-level strike aircraft.

The Group was commanded by Colonel Clinton C. Wasem, and he had decided that his pilots were ready for their first mission on 25th April, which was nothing more threatening than a fighter sweep along the French coast. During the four months that the 474th operated from Warmwell it completed 108 missions but lost 27 aircraft in the process. Three of these were lost on 7th May when the pilots were escorting B-26s on a bombing operation; however, two of the pilots baled out, and one, Lieutenant Thatcher, managed to evade capture and returned to this country via Spain and Gibraltar. On 5th/6th June the P-38s provided fighter cover for the invasion convoys; it was said that the P-38s were selected for this task because of their distinctive shapes being unlike any Luftwaffe aircraft, and therefore less likely to attract 'friendly' fire! Two pilots were lost and it was thought that their aircraft had collided. For about the next week the P-38 Groups continued their covering role over the Channel, before being released for bombing sorties in support of the ground troops.

Perhaps the highlight of the Group's operations from Warmwell came on 18th July, when they were led by Lieutenant Colonel Henry Darling, the Group's Executive Officer. It was a good day for the Group with ten Fw 190s destroyed for the loss of three P-38s; two pilots escaped with the third killed. Another three pilots were lost before the Group left

The fine memorial stone at Crossways.

Warmwell. This was the last of the Ninth's 18 Fighter Groups to move across to France. The pilots completed their last mission from Warmwell on 5th August and on the following day the main party moved to Neuilly airfield, about 70 miles to the south-west of Paris; later in the month (the 26th) the Group was to gain a Distinguished Unit Citation for its ground attacks against enemy troops in the Falaise/Argentan area.

In August the airfield was handed back to the RAF and on the 27th of the month No 17 Armament Practice Camp moved in from Southend to provide gunnery training for the numerous squadrons of the 2TAF. In November No 14 APC also arrived at Warmwell, and for the next twelve months a considerable number of Spitfire and Typhoon squadrons arrived from advanced landing grounds on the Continent, and stayed at Warmwell for about two weeks; some, such as Nos 174, 175, 257, 350 and 402, were making return visits to the airfield.

It could be said that Warmwell had now completed a full circle, the airfield was operating once again as it had been back in pre-war days. The two Practice Camps were disbanded in October 1945 and in the following month the airfield was placed on a Care and Maintenance basis. It was finally sold in 1950 and has since disappeared under gravel extraction workings and housing development. However, in June 1989, a fine memorial stone on the village green at Crossways was dedicated to all the Allied airmen that served at the airfield from 1937 to 1946.

8

CIVILIANS
AT WAR

At six o'clock on the first evening of the war, HM King George VI made a broadcast to the Empire. His shy and hesitant manner, allied to his distressing stammer, seemed to give his words greater moment and sincerity. 'In this grave hour, perhaps the most fateful in our history . . . For the second time in the lives of most of us, we are at war . . . There may be dark days ahead and war can no longer be confined to the battlefield . . . we must be ready for whatever service and sacrifice it may demand, then with God's help, we shall prevail.' A copy of the King's message was sent to every household in the land.

Most people little realised then just how heavy their trials and burdens would be in the coming war, and how the next six years would dramatically change their lives – every man, woman, and child in the country. The conflict would soon become known as the 'People's War', or, as Winston Churchill preferred to call it, 'a war of the unknown warriors'; it should be borne in mind that only about 10% of the total population would serve in the armed forces. Those who lived through the long ordeal, whatever their ages at the time, have their own special recollections of the war - the wail of the air-raid sirens, the incessant drone of aircraft overhead, searchlights, air-raid shelters, barrage balloons, bombing, food rationing, blackout, evacuation, gas masks, endless queues, *ITMA*, BBC news broadcasts, the Home Guard, GIs . . .

War Declared! (Daily Telegraph)

indeed, the list seems endless, and each can still evoke vivid memories of those wartime days.

Many can recall that sunny but fateful Sunday, 3rd September 1939, when Neville Chamberlain, the Prime Minister, had gravely informed the Nation that it was now at war with Germany, and most were 'relieved that something *definite* has happened at last'. However, the majority felt that the war had really started two days earlier when in the early hours of 1st September German troops had entered Poland; they then knew that their fate and future was sealed. ARP (Air Raid Precautions) wardens and members of the Auxiliary Fire Service were mobilised, the BBC merged its National and Regional networks into a single Home Service, and the Blackout regulations came into force from sunset. But perhaps the most ominous sign of the coming conflict was the mass evacuation of children mainly from London and other cities that began at sunrise.

The most evocative and poignant images of the war were the sight of thousands upon thousands of children with attached labels, carrying their gas masks in small cardboard boxes, and their few precious possessions packed in battered cases or carrier bags. This mass evacuation was described as 'an exodus bigger than Moses . . . like the movement of ten armies'. The plans for this momentous and quite remarkable operation had been put in hand earlier in the year, when it was expected that more than 3½ million would be relocated, although the actual number was less than 1½ million . . . over 800,000 schoolchildren, 520,000 mothers and children under school age, and 103,000 teachers and helpers.

Dorset was considered to be a prime reception area. Billeting officers had been appointed, local reception centres established in the towns, and in Dorchester Rural District alone, it had been decided that over 4,600 evacuees could be accommodated, whereas West Moors was told to expect some 2,000 children mainly from Portsmouth. Other than the billeting of children and families in private homes (at the rate of 8s 6d per head per week), one of the biggest problems was the provision of adequate schooling and within a week or so a shift system had been introduced with local children attending in the morning and evacuees in the afternoon. Mostly the evacuees came from London, though there were still a number that had been moved from nearby Southampton and Portsmouth. By the spring of 1940 almost three quarters had left for

The importance of Air Raid Precautions can be seen in these cigarette cards issued by W.D. & H. O. Wills in 1938.

home, although many would return later in the year as the night blitz intensified. All those households that gave shelter to evacuees would ultimately receive a letter of thanks for 'a work of great value' from HM The Queen.

One of the major consequences of the 'People's War' was the movement of people. In addition to those who were officially evacuated, many more made their own private arrangements with relatives or friends, and well over one million were forced to move because their homes were destroyed or heavily damaged; after just six weeks of bombing in the autumn of 1940 over a quarter of a million people were reported to be homeless. During the whole of the war, it was estimated that there were in excess of 60 million changes of addresses in a total civilian population of some 34 million.

For the rest of that September the British people were beginning to come to terms with the major changes to their everyday lives. A plethora of Government intructions were issued concerning the procedures to be followed during air raids and gas attacks, and the special arrangements for schools. Although places of entertainment were closed at first, within a week cinemas and theatres were allowed to reopen. However, it was the blackout that was the most immediate inconvenience, and initially gave rise to considerable annoyance; there was a marked increase in the number of road accidents and minor injuries to pedestrians and cyclists. In November the 'Safety First Association' estimated that 'in a three years' war 40,000 people will have died as a result of this attempt to protect the civil population against enemy aircraft'. A writer to The Times thought that 'this remedy [the blackout] may turn out to be worse than the disease.' The ARP wardens on their regular 'lights' patrols could be a little over-zealous at times in ensuring that the blackout was complete. 'Put that light out' became an all too familiar cry! The blackout was never really accepted, a vast majority considered it to be the most irksome wartime restriction and inconvenience, more so even than food rationing.

Perhaps the other most abiding memory to come from the first month of the war was the gas mask. Nobody who has ever worn one, if only during the seemingly endless and regular practice drills, has ever forgotten the chilling experience – the clammy breathlessness they induced and the sharp and very distinctive smell of rubber and disinfectant. Everybody was 'compelled' to carry them, although less than one in five actually took them to work, and the ARP wardens did not endear themselves to the rest of the civilian population by their rather officious manner whilst attempting to enforce the official edict. The Government considered that the threat of poison gas attacks was very real, posters were prominently displayed and the tops of post boxes were coated with a special yellow gas detector paint.

Petrol rationing was introduced on 22nd September, the first ominous sign of things to come, although this affected only a small percentage of the population as just one family in ten had use of a car. Five days later the first War Budget was presented, which brought a sharp increase in Income Tax to 7s 6d in the £1 with additions to the duties on beer, spirits, wines, tobacco and sugar. In the coming years taxation would increase dramatically, but it would be borne with a calm and almost resigned stoicism by the public, because 'after all, this war must be paid for.' Perhaps the almost total lack of consumer goods in the shops made the punitive rates of taxation a little easier to bear, as there was precious little for the public to buy with their hard-earned wages.

National Registration Day was set for 29th September and the establishment of a National Register enabled the Government to issue to every person a buff-coloured National Identity Card with a personal number. The card had to be 'carefully preserved' and produced on demand to 'persons who are authorised by law'. The establishment of the Register brought the introduction of food rationing that much closer. The Identity Card and Ration Book became the two most important civilian documents of the war, but nobody would have predicted that Ration Books would still be in use 14 years later!

The urgency to make over all available land to the cultivation of food saw the introduction of the insistent wartime motto, 'Dig for Victory'. The Minister of Agriculture, Sir Reginald Dorman, demanded that all gardens be given over to the cultivation of vegetables, and also that every family should take on an allotment. Helped by the introduction of Double British Summer Time in May 1941 horticulture became a national pastime, as indeed did the rearing of chickens. By 1943 the number of allotments had doubled to almost 1½ million.

As one inveterate wartime diarist recorded, 'we have slipped very easily into war habits.' Of course this had been made easier by what had become known as the 'Phoney' or 'Bore' war. The aerial bombardment had not materialised, and there seemed to be a decided lack of wartime

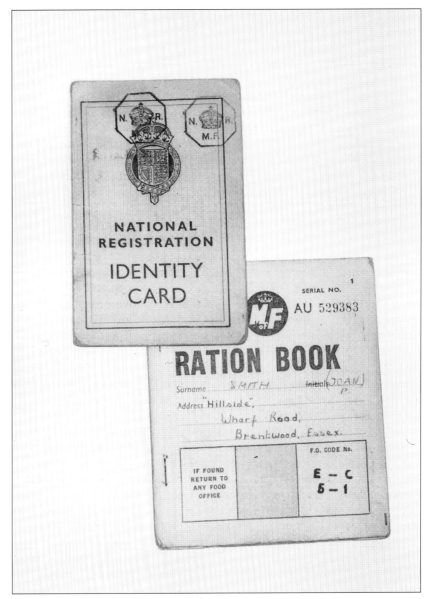

The two most important documents of the Home Front during the war.

activity anywhere. This strange and unreal situation brought about a general unease and uncertainty in the country with everybody waiting in dread for 'the balloon to go up'. The winter of 1939/40 proved to be the most severe of the century, with weeks of hard frosts and heavy snowfalls, and although coal was not rationed it was nevertheless in short supply because of transport problems caused by the severe weather. Food rationing had been first introduced in November, and was extended in early January; the habit of queuing for food, buses, films etc became ingrained in the public. The cynics would say, 'If you see a queue, join it'! For the majority of the people who lived through this first depressing wartime winter, all would later agree that it was probably the worst period of the war. The uncertainty of what the future held only added to their malaise and discomfort.

BBC radio became the country's chief solace during these dark and cold winter days. The news bulletins had settled into a regular pattern, and they became an essential fund of information; indeed communal listening, especially to the essential nine o'clock news, became a feature of the times. From June 1940 the newsreaders identified themselves. Alvar Lidell, Frank Phillips, Stuart Hibberd, John Snagge, Wilfred Pickles and Bruce Belfrage became celebrities, as did the novelist and playwriter J. B. Priestley for his 'homely fireside chats', which had a regular audience of ten million. But it was the comedy shows such as *Band Wagon*, *Hi Gang*, and *It's That Man Again* (later *ITMA*) that became firm favourites, bringing some humour into the drab and dreary wartime years. In 1942 over 16 million listened to *ITMA*'s fifth series and Tommy Handley and the programme's various characters, Mrs Mopp, Colonel Chinstrap, Funf the spy, passed into radio (or wireless) folklore.

Suddenly the harsh winter gave way to a bright and early spring and during Easter (at the end of March) people flocked to the coast, as they had always done in pre-war days, but it was almost as if they had a premonition that this would be the last 'peaceful' holiday of the war. On 4th April, Neville Chamberlain made a most ill-considered speech, in the light of following events. 'After seven months of war I feel ten times as confident of victory as I did at the beginning . . . one thing is certain, Hitler has missed the bus'! Four days later Denmark and Norway were invaded and the 'Phoney War' or 'The Strangest of Wars' (as Chamberlain had described it) had come to an abrupt end. On the last day of the month the first fatalities occurred as a result of enemy air

Winston Churchill on one of his visits to Dorset in July 1940. He is being greeted by Lieutenant General Brooke. (Imperial War Museum)

attack at a most unlikely place – the popular seaside resort of Clacton-on-Sea in Essex; over 50 houses were damaged and there were 162 civilian casualties with two deaths. The 'People's War' was about to begin with a vengeance.

On 10th May the tired and broken Neville Chamberlain was forced to resign (he died in November) and he was replaced by Winston Churchill, who was now in charge of an all-party National Government, the formation of which only emphasised the perilous state of the country. The arrival at the helm of this inspiring and charismatic war leader proved to be a matter of 'Cometh the hour, cometh the man'. From his very first speech as Prime Minister, which he preferred to call 'broadcasts', he said that he had nothing to offer but 'blood, toil, sweat and tears'. He had the innate ability to greatly inspire the country through its darkest days, he was able to express the feelings of the British people in stirring and unforgettable words. Wherever he went in the country, he was universally feted and cheered. His hallmarks were the black Homburg hat, the inevitable cigar and the V for Victory sign, and 'Winnie' epitomised the 'bulldog spirit' of the country. Throughout the coming years no less than 78% of the public approved of his conduct of the war.

Within weeks of becoming Prime Minister, Churchill flew from Warmwell (on 31st May) to Paris to have urgent talks with the French Government. Then in July he was again in Dorset inspecting Southern Command, and he visited the coastal defences at Poole and Sandbanks, as well as anti-aircraft batteries. Later, in April 1942, Churchill visited Lulworth Camp to see the new armoured tanks that bore his name. He would also visit the county in April 1944 to witness the preparations for D-Day.

Within four days of Churchill coming to power, his new Secretary of State for War, Anthony Eden, announced the formation of a volunteer force, to be known as the LDV or the Local Defence Volunteers. Within 24 hours of the radio appeal by Eden for men between the ages of 17 and 65 years to enlist for this new force, over ¼ million had come forward to register at local police stations, and by the end of June this figure had risen to over one million. They would not be paid, but would be provided with a uniform and armed (ultimately!), and would be required to serve a minimum of ten hours per week. However, at first they received little more than their 'LDV' armbands, these initials were jokingly said to be short for 'Look, Duck and Vanish'! Soon almost every town and village in the county had their own platoon, for example Alderholt had 32 recruits, who made the village hall their headquarters. The various battalions were commanded by retired senior Army officers – the 'Colonel Blimps' – and in the early days 75% of the Home Guard were ex-servicemen. Ultimately there were seven battalions in the county.

In August the LDV was renamed the Home Guard, at the strong insistence of Churchill despite opposition from Eden and Service chiefs, and slowly under Viscount Bridgeman, DSO, MC, the Director-General, the Home Guard was placed on a more military footing. Weapons were rather scarce until one million First World War rifles were purchased from the United States. The force's primary function was to deal with any enemy airborne troops that landed and they took their duty very seriously. In the early days they could be somewhat over-zealous in their nightly activities, and there were many instances of 'trigger happy' volunteers shooting first and asking questions afterwards! Home

Guardsmen also manned road-blocks, patrolled their area of control and inspected the Identity Cards of persons moving during the hours of darkness. For this reason they were often referred to as the 'Army of the Night'. By the summer of 1943 there were over 1,100 battalions throughout the country comprising some 1¾ million men with an average age of under 30 years.

Contrary to the comic images created by television's *Dad's Army*, the Home Guard became a quite professional force, manning anti-aircraft batteries as well as undertaking army duties later in the war. Over 130 medals were awarded to Home Guardsmen including two George Crosses, said to be the 'Civilian's Victoria Cross'. The Home Guard was a unique experiment that became a tremendous success, costing the Government only about £9 per man per year. Perhaps its greatest contribution was that by its very presence in such large numbers it enabled regular soldiers be released for other war service.

With the fall of France in June 1940, most people were convinced that an invasion was imminent, more a case of *when* rather than *if*. This general feeling of impending disaster had not been helped by the issue to every household of *Rules for Civilians in case of Invasion*. This pamphlet gave instructions to 'stay indoors . . . hide maps, food, petrol and bicycles . . . ' and furthermore they were cautioned, 'Do not panic . . . and await further instructions'! A letter in *The Times* of 24th May suggested that, 'If all signposts, milestones and AA notices giving the names of villages were removed until after the war, it would be inconvenient for us, but it would be more than inconvenient for the enemy landing by parachute . . .' In the following month road signs were removed as were the names on railway stations, and maps and guides were withdrawn from sale. From 13th June church bells were ordered to be silenced, only to be rung as a warning that the expected paratroops had landed.

Like all other coastal counties Dorset had a coastal belt designated as a Defence Area. 'Dragon's teeth' anti-tank obstacles, pillboxes, concrete road blocks, and anti-glider poles were erected. Barbed wire and iron girder defences were placed along the beaches, and as one Bournemouth resident later recalled, 'You could not swim but you could paddle'. During the immediate period of the invasion scare, the coastal towns and shores had severely restricted access with control posts and special 'Military Control' passes being issued to local residents. Curfews were imposed and most, if not all, sea-front hotels and guest-houses had been requistioned. In the first week of July the central sections of Bournemouth and Boscombe piers were blown up to prevent them from being used by enemy forces. Dorset was now well and truly in the frontline.

The dire situation just across the other side of the Channel was brought home to the locals when, in May, some 3,000 Dutch refugees arrived at Poole Harbour, and were temporarily housed on Brownsea Island, whilst they and their papers were examined before being allowed entry into the country. In the following month some tattered remnants of the French army landed at Weymouth, and according to reports they 'appeared to be more like refugees than fighting troops'; they were taken to Bournemouth for a period of recuperation. Later in the month Weymouth was the port of arrival of over 29,000 Channel Islanders fleeing from the impending German occupation of the Islands.

Such a large and steady influx of refugees only fuelled the country's deep concern about enemy agents. Without doubt the country was gripped by a 'spy mania'. All foreigners were treated with the gravest suspicion, posters carrying such slogans as 'Careless talk costs lives' and 'Be like Dad, Keep Mum' could be seen everywhere, even the carrying of cameras could lead to instant arrest. Ed Murrow, the famous American broadcaster, recalled the time when he was arrested as a foreign spy because 'I asked too many questions about wartime life in the country at a time when everybody was looking for spies.'

The country had been preparing itself for the 'threat from the air' since well before the outbreak of war. Brick public shelters had been built, though initially the number that were provided would only accommodate about 10% of the total population. Emergency water tanks, brick-built ARP warden and First Aid posts had been erected in surburban streets, and important buildings in town centres were now protected by sandbags.

Private air-raid shelters had been offered to all households at the cost of £7 but free to those with an annual income less than £250. These shelters were of a curved corrugated sheet design, intended to be sunk several feet into the ground, and then covered with earth or sandbags, and were designed to shelter six persons. They became known as 'Anderson' shelters supposedly from Sir John Anderson (later Lord Waverley), who in 1938 had been in charge of the Nation's Civil Defence preparations, although their name was actually derived from their original designer, Dr David A. Anderson. One historian wrote, 'To be inside an Anderson shelter felt rather like being entombed in a small, dark bicycle shed, smelling of earth and damp.' However, they were acceptably safe and were able to withstand considerable blast damage except for a direct hit, which according to one official handout 'was very unlikely to happen'!

When the Government discovered that many families would not use the outdoor garden shelters, and preferred to stay indoors, maybe sheltering in understairs cupboards or basements, it introduced, in the autumn of 1941, an indoor iron shelter with steel mesh sides – the Morrison - which also doubled as a table. It was named after Herbert Morrison, who had taken over the Civil Defence responsibilities. By November 1941 over ½ million Morrison shelters had been issued, but nevertheless it was the Anderson shelter that became an affectionate symbol of the wartime days.

By June 1940 it was disclosed that well over a third of the population had not taken air-raid precautions of any description despite a quite massive publicity campaign by the Ministry of Information. Some of the relatively simple and recommended preventive measures that could be made with little cost or effort were: the application of paper strips to protect windows from bomb blast; the provision of buckets of sand/earth and water for incendiary bombs; making-up a rudimentary first-aid kit, a stirrup pump to be kept handy, attics cleared as an anti-incendiary measure; and a stock of vital food supplies collected. Not until the autumn of 1940 as the night blitz intensified did many families decide to take these and other air-raid precautions seriously.

Although a single incendiary bomb was dropped on the Royal Naval Cordite Factory at Holton Heath on 24th April, and Portland's first air raid came on 30th June, it was in July (earlier than many areas of the country) that Dorset really began to suffer at the hands of the Luftwaffe. From this month onwards the air-raid sirens continually sounded their ululating and shrieking tones, becoming an almost daily and nightly fear. The doleful and dreaded fluctuating wail of the 'Red Warning' or 'Raiders Approach', which orginally lasted for two minutes, followed some hours later by the blessed, steady and continuous sound of the 'All Clear' or 'Raiders Passed', had become a frightening feature of everyday life. For instance, at Portland the siren was sounded 784 times and at

Christchurch on over 950 occasions, the last in July 1944. The sirens were often referred to as the 'Wailing Winnies', although one wartime poet wrote of them as, 'Whoohoo go the goblins, coming back at nightfall'. Of course most of the villages did not have air-raid sirens, their alarm system consisted of ARP wardens cycling around the village blowing short blasts on their whistles, then much later long blasts to signify the 'All Clear'.

On 12th June the large coal hulk *Himalaya* was sunk by bombing in Portland Harbour; this vessel, when launched in 1853, was the world's largest ship. Then on the night of 3rd/4th July Bournemouth received its first air raid, when one house was set on fire and several others damaged. During the daylight hours of the 4th the Royal Naval base at Portland came under heavy attack from Junkers 87s. Leading Seaman Jack Mantle was posthumously awarded the Victoria Cross for remaining at the starboard 'pom-pom' even though mortally wounded when his anti-aircraft ship, HMS *Foylebank*, was severely bombed and sunk. Mantle was the first naval rating to be awarded the VC in the war, and he is buried at the Royal Naval Cemetery at Portland. Over 170 seamen were killed in this raid along with six civilians.

For almost the next twelve months most of the county would suffer air raids to a lesser and greater extent, with Bournemouth, Poole, Portland, Weymouth and Christchurch being frequently targeted. But even the inland country areas were not immune. A villager at Toller Fratrum, some miles north-west of Dorchester, well remembered Good Friday 1941 as 'a terrible, terrible night, never will I forget it. The Home Guard unit thought we were no more.'

The lovely and ancient town of Sherborne suffered harshly in the late afternoon of 30th September when it was reported that in just three minutes of mayhem 300 bombs had fallen on and around the town. The damage was considerable, almost 45% of the town's buildings were either demolished or damaged, 18 people died, including a youngster who had only been evacuated from London the previous day, and 32 people sustained injuries and were detained in hospital. It was the worst wartime raid on an inland town in Dorset. And yet the following day a furniture store in Cheap Street, which had been extensively damaged, carried this notice: 'We have been bombed, buggered and bewildered, but business as usual'! Thus echoing the same determined message that could be seen in all bombed cities and towns during the blitz of 1940/1.

200

A Miss Maud Steele, supervisor of the Sherborne telephone exchange, remained at her post throughout the raid and was awarded the George Cross, which had only been instigated six days previously.

On 16th November Bournemouth suffered its heaviest air raid so far, when 53 people were killed and over 2,000 properties damaged. Then in March 1941 the Bourne Valley Gasworks at Poole was bombed at lunchtime and 34 workers died with another 23 injured.

But 'death from the air' could also take on another form. The crashes of both friendly and enemy aircraft brought an additional hazard to the civilian population; this was especially so whilst the Battle of Britain raged overhead. From April 1940 to the end of the year over 70 aircraft (almost half of them Luftwaffe) came to grief at various spots in the county, though they were mostly confined to the countryside with no resultant civilian casualties. On two days during this period, 25th August and 27th September, no fewer than 13 Me 109s and 110s crashed in Dorset, as well as four RAF fighters. And on 25th September, two Heinkel 111s came down in the county – one at Branksome Park and the other at Studland.

The winter of 1940/1, notable for its severe weather, was a time, according to a wartime diarist, when 'Sleep is now elevated to a position of national importance'. Most of the male civilian population was engaged in some kind of volunteer Civil Defence work – ARP wardens, rescue workers, special policemen, auxiliary firemen, ambulance drivers, fire watchers etc – or served in the Royal Observer Corps, and after their onerous and tiring night duties, which afforded little opportunity for rest, the following morning they were back at their daytime labours either in the factories, shops or offices.

With the advantage of hindsight 1941 can be considered as the nadir of the country's fortunes. By the end of the year over 40,000 civilians had been killed in air raids with another 50,000 injured; not until the following year was it possible to say that 'the enemy had killed more soldiers and airmen than women and children.' Without doubt the 'Home Front', as the politicians liked to describe it, was bearing the brunt of the war. With the Battle of the Atlantic reaching a critical stage, many goods disappeared from shops and food rationing became more stringent. Although bread was never rationed, the white loaf became a thing of the past to be replaced by the National Wheatmeal loaf, which was universally detested. Towards the end of the year a points system

*1st October 1940: the scene of devastation in Half Moon Street, Sherborne.
(Sherborne Museum)*

was introduced for canned goods, and the purchase of clothing and footwear was severely curtailed by the use of coupons – at first 48 per month. It is interesting to note that back in October 1940 the Board of Trade had requisitioned the Carlton Hotel on the East Cliff at Bournemouth to accommodate its civil servants engaged on the food and clothing rationing schemes. In such a climate of shortages and utter austerity the Black Market flourished and 'spivs' were born; individuals who could provide anything from petrol and clothing coupons to scarce consumer goods and foodstuffs, but at a price.

As the year came to a close, conscription for unmarried women between the ages of 20 and 30 years was introduced, and they were given the option of either serving in the women's auxiliary armed services, Civil Defence, the Land Army or industry. Members of the Women's Auxiliary Air Force, which had been formed in June 1939, served at the RAF stations in the county as well as operating at most of the barrage balloon sites throughout Dorset, as were WRNS at Portland, Weymouth and Poole. Already thousands of women were engaged in filling jobs vacated by men called up for military service. They worked on the buses, and railways, as well as delivering the milk and post. By mid-1943 the number of women engaged in full-time war work was well in excess of three million, most of them employed in the aircraft and munitions factories. This huge increase in the employment of women was perhaps one of the major social changes brought about by the war.

The most conspicuous female war workers in Dorset were the girls of the Women's Land Army. The organisation had been founded in 1917 but was revived by Lady Gertrude Denman in June 1939, who later wrote, 'The Land Army fights in the fields. It is in the fields of Britain that the most critical battle of the present war may well be fought and won.' The Land Army girls had a distinctive uniform – green jumper and tie, fawn corduroy knee breeches, thick wool socks, an officer-style greatcoat, and brown felt hat. All were volunteers; the girls could join at the age of 17 years, and came from all walks of life, but over one third hailed either from London or the northern industrial cities. After about a month's training, the girls were usually sent to one of the many hostels dotted throughout the county. Their hours were long and the work was hard and rather poorly paid, indeed the recruitment posters were criticised for portraying an idealised picture of life on the land, quite contrary to the reality. Their public image was not particularly high,

203

Heinkel 111 brought down at Westfield Farm, Studland on 25th September 1940. (Muse

Army Flying)

often they were disparagingly called 'sod busters' and they had to face considerable suspicion from farmers before ultimately gaining their grudging respect. At its peak, in 1943, the WLA numbered over 87,000 and it survived well after the war, being finally disbanded in October 1950.

However, since the outbreak of the war women had taken up voluntary war work, in the Civil Defence, the Red Cross and the Women's Voluntary Service; the latter attracting the highest number. By 1941 there were over one million WVS workers. It could be said that the Service was essentially middle class, with its uniform of grey-green tweed, felt hat and beetroot-red jumper. Throughout the war they made an immense contribution, often operating under most trying and difficult conditions. Known universally to the public and servicemen alike as 'the women in green', they operated canteens, reception and rest centres for servicemen, and were engaged in helping bombed and homeless families; indeed, no task seemed too difficult or onerous for these ladies, they were another essential adjunct to the Home Front.

The National Savings Movement was one of the success stories of the Second World War. It had started back in November 1939 as the War Savings Scheme, which aimed to collect some £475 million in a year. The start of regular and on-going National Savings became an outright winner, with savings groups being formed in every street, office, factory and school. It was said that at least 25% of the average weekly income was given up to savings compared with a mere 5% before the war. But the most dramatic achievements of the movement were the special drives organised annually on a national basis, from the Spitfire Fund in the summer of 1940 through War Weapons Week, Warships, and Wings for Victory to Salute the Soldier Week in 1944. Special plaques were issued to local authorities to recognise worthy attainments in these weeks. Several towns in the county had Spitfires named after them as a result of their contributions, such as *Villae de Poole*, *Bournemouth II Crest* and *The Brit*. Wimborne and Cranborne District Councils were called upon, in 1941, to make an independent savings effort of £55,000 towards the cost of a corvette to be named HMS *Challenger*, and they were engaged in a friendly rivalry with St Thomas in Devon. In 1942 the county started a massive savings appeal to raise funds to replace the cruiser HMS *Dorsetshire* (which had sunk in April 1942), with an original target of £2.7 million, although by January 1943 the fund had reached over £3 million.

The National Savings Movement was just the most publicised manifestation of a saving compulsion that gripped the nation throughout the war years. The public was continually exhorted by the Government to save everything from rags, bones, jam jars, glass, rubber, waste food and waste paper to old pots and pans, books and newspapers. 'Waste Not Want Not' and 'Make Do and Mend' were the all-important precepts, and the guiding symbol of this era of thriftiness and frugality was the 'Squander Bug', a cartoon figure liberally covered in German swastikas which appeared in newspapers, magazines and posters. Salvage drives were organised from street level upwards, with schoolchildren eagerly involved in the various collections. By the end of the war some six million tons of salvage had been collected, the majority of it scrap metal. Iron railings around buildings, houses and parks had been amongst the first to disappear for scrap.

The 'Battle of Fuel', as it was described, was an wartime on-going operation and the country was urged to follow the King's example and use no more than five inches of hot water in their baths! They were also continually exhorted to consider, 'Is my journey really necessary?', though quite honestly, few people would want to use the vastly over-crowded, irregular and unpunctual trains, unless their journeys were really essential!

As the country entered the fourth year of war, HM King George VI appointed 3rd September 1942 as a day of prayer, marked with religious services throughout the country. Rather appropriately factories, shops and offices stopped work for a quarter of an hour at 11 am for a broadcast service; most felt that the war had already lasted an eternity, and there seemed to be precious little to celebrate. However, by October, the situation had changed with the first land victory of the war – El Alamein. Winston Churchill was cautious in his praise: 'This is not the end. It is not even the beginning of the end. But it is, perhaps, the end of the beginning.' On 15th November church bells rang out again to celebrate the victory, so perhaps at long last there was the merest glimmer of light at the end of a very long tunnel, and after all 'the Yanks had arrived', although it would be awhile before they made their presence felt in Dorset.

During 1943 there was said to be 'a perceptible air of optimism in the country'. The news from the various war fronts was much more encouraging and would steadily improve during the year. The Ministry

Wimborne Home Guard marching in the procession to mark Warship Week,
November 1941. (The Priest's House Museum)

Collection of iron railings from Poole Park. (Poole Museum Service)

of Food, under the ebullient Lord Woolton, the most famous wartime politician after Churchill, was able to report that the nation's diet was now healthier and better than it had been pre-war, despite the fact that food rationing was again tightened. The improvement was largely due to a vast increase in home food production, but also the numerous works, office and school canteens which had opened were not so restricted by food rationing. Another factor was the introduction of 'communal feeding centres', or British Restaurants as they were known. They were non-profitmaking and Government sponsored, providing a good and wholesome mid-day meal for one shilling per head, and staffed by volunteer workers. Most towns in the county had one, if not more, British Restaurants and they certainly eased the problems of eking out the very meagre weekly food rations for the hard-pressed housewives.

Not everything on the Home Front was favourable; on 23rd May Bournemouth suffered its most damaging air raid of the war, when on a Sunday lunchtime a low-level attack by Fw 190s bombed the centre of the town, leaving in their wake over 3,000 buildings damaged, and 77 persons killed (including a number of Canadian servicemen). The town would suffer two further air raids later in the year. It was not until the following May that the last bombs fell on the county, at Bournemouth on the 27th of month, followed the next day by an air raid on Weymouth, when its hospital sustained damage and four persons were killed and another 13 injured.

In September 1943 as the country entered upon its fifth year of the war, the British people were, as a wartime diarist recorded, 'eagerly hungering for the opening of a Second Front [the invasion of mainland Europe], and bets are being taken in offices and pubs as to when this long-awaited event will happen'. However, those living in the county would soon see very real evidence that the 'Second Front' was indeed coming closer.

The many Army camps in Dorset ensured that the locals had become quite used to the presence of servicemen in their midst, but even this did not prepare them for the massive 'invasion' of American troops in 1944, which would create the greatest upheaval of the war. The county virtually became a gigantic American camp and vehicle park. The first arrivals were engineers to build the hutted and tented camps (twelve), the hospitals (seven), supply depôts, fuel and ammunition dumps, and port facilities. It was the US 1st Infantry Division and its support units that would make Dorset their temporary home in the months before D-Day. The Division, known as the 'Big Red One' from its shoulder patch of a red '1' on a green background, had fought in North Africa and Sicily, and had arrived in Britain in November 1943. The Division and its units would be spread throughout Dorset, hardly a corner would escape the 'Friendly Invasion'. The ports of Weymouth and Portland, which the Americans called 'the biggest little port in the world', were re-allocated to the US Naval Units, with Poole also having a strong American presence.

Soon the country roads would be choked with the American heavy trucks and the little omnipresent jeeps, and it was perhaps not surprising that the accident rate rose alarmingly. All the towns from Bridport in the west to Bournemouth in the east, and Shaftesbury in the north, would become crowded with American troops and echo to their strange accents. The GIs proceeded to take over the public houses, cinemas and dance halls, and quite naturally there was a certain resentment at first, their brashness, confidence and, at times, seeming

Locals and GIs meet at the Dove Inn, Burton Bradstock, Dorset. (Imperial War Museum)

arrogance were difficult to bear. The very fact that they were well paid, and had ready access to all manner of goods that had long since disappeared from shops did not help matters. However, soon understanding prevailed and their friendly and generous nature thawed most of the local reserve. During the Christmas of 1943 their sincere kindness and magnanimity to local children was very evident.

Each Dorset town had at least one American Red Cross Club where coffee, doughnuts, cigarettes, newspapers and other facilities were provided, and they also hosted many dances. Bournemouth became the mecca for US servicemen with its cinemas, theatres and restaurants as the main attraction, and several large hotels had been requisitioned as American rest centres. But it was at the local public houses, of which there was no equivalent in the United States, that the two different cultures met, and they became the favourite places of recreation for the 'Yanks'. Although they had initially complained about 'the warm, flat and weak beer', they quickly acquired a taste for it, which in itself caused certain problems with the locals because for most of the war

Bound for France: American troops marching to their port of embarkation; note the car driver giving the 'V for Victory' sign. (Imperial War Museum)

supplies of beer were strictly rationed! Certainly it could be said that the Americans brought a touch of glamour to wartime austerity Britain; as one Blandford resident recently recalled, 'I still remember the Yanks almost more than I do the war'!

Unlike other areas of the country where Eighth Air Force units remained in the same locale for a number of years, strong and abiding links with the local communities are not so evident. Nevertheless for the relatively brief period that they remained in Dorset, they certainly left their mark; perhaps not too surprising considering that over ½ million American troops passed through the county on their way to France. There are two memorials to mark these momentous events; one at Victoria Gardens, Fortuneswell, Portland unveiled on 22nd August 1945, and the other on Weymouth Esplanade, opposite the Royal Hotel, which served as the port's D-Day embarkation headquarters.

It was the familiar voice of John Snagge that announced the historic news at 9.30 am on 6th June 1944: 'D-Day has come. Early this morning the Allies began the assault on the north-western face of Hitler's

Memorial on Weymouth Esplanade to the US troops that left from Weymouth and Portland Harbours. The light at the top is never extinguished.

The snack bar at the American Red Cross Club, Bridport, 1944.
(via Mrs L. P. Puley)

European fortress'. According to reports there was 'an almost tangible release of tension in the country'. Dorset was fortunate in being too far west to suffer from the V1 rocket onslaught that started in mid-June, it did however bring about a fresh mini evacuation.

During the autumn things on the Home Front were just beginning to return to some semblance of normality. The strict blackout regulations were partially lifted to universal approval, and at the beginning of November the Home Guard was stood down, with the Guardsmen parading for a final time in early December. Christmas 1944 was a time, at long last, for modest celebration; extra rations of sweets, sugar, margarine and meat had been allowed, and the clear, bright and sunny weather seemed to reflect the optimistic mood of the country. With the coming of spring, there was a rising tide of belief that the long and hard fight was fast coming to a conclusion. The BBC news bulletins were followed with even greater interest as they chronicled the Allied armies' steady advance into Germany. Then, on 2nd May, came the announcement that the British public had been waiting to hear– 'Hitler died yesterday in Berlin' – six days later the war in Europe was over.

Every street, village and town in the country celebrated VE Day on 8th May with thanksgiving services, victory parades, parties, bonfires, firework displays, fancy dress parades and sports events, with the celebrations continuing well into the early morning. One newspaper commented that the celebrations were more 'a conscious sense of relief from strain rather than a triumphant exultant.'

After almost six long years of unremitting hardship, privation and sacrifice the 'People's War' had come to an end, but at a heavy cost – more than 60,000 killed with another 86,000 seriously injured and well over 2 million made homeless. As was usual Winston Churchill found the appropriate words at the right time. On the evening of 8th May he addressed the large and jubilant crowd that had gathered in Whitehall. 'God bless you all. This is *your* victory – the victory of the cause of freedom in every land. In all our long history we have never seen a greater day than this.'

BIBLIOGRAPHY

During my research I consulted various books. I list them below with my grateful thanks to the authors.

Air Historical Branch, *The Rise & Fall of the German Air Force, 1933–1945*, Arms & Armour Press, 1983.

Air Ministry, *The Battle of Britain*, HMSO, 1941.

Armitage, Michael, *The Royal Air Force: An Illustrated History*, Cassell, 1993.

Ashley, Harry, *The Dorset Coast*, Countryside Books, 1992.

Ashworth, Chris, *Action Stations: No 5 Military Airfields of the South West*, PSL, 1982.

Ashworth, Chris, *RAF Coastal Command*, PSL, 1992.

Bowyer, Chas, *Fighter Command: 1936–1968*, Dent, 1980.

Bowyer, Michael J.F., *Aircraft for the Many*, PSL, 1995.

Calder, Angus, *The People's War: Britain 1939–1945*, Pimlico, 1992.

Cobham, Sir Alan, *A Time to Fly*, Shepheard Walwyn, 1978.

Croall, Jonathan, *Don't You Know There's a War On?: the People's Voice*, Hutchinson, 1989.

Cruddas, Colin, *In Cobham's Company: Sixty Years of Flight Refuelling Limited*, Cobham plc, 1994.

Dawson, Leslie, *Wings over Dorset: Aviation's Story in the South*, Dorset Pub. Co., 2nd Revised Ed., 1989.

Deighton, Len, *Fighter: The True Story of the Battle of Britain*, J. Cape, 1977.

Delve, Ken, *D-Day: The Air Battle*, Arms & Armour, 1994.

Forty, George, *Frontline Dorset: A County at War, 1939–45*, Dorset Books, 1994.

Franks, Norman L. R., *Fighter Command, 1936–1968*, Patrick Stephens, 1992.

Franks, Norman, *The Greatest Air Battle: Dieppe 19th August 1942*, Grub Street, 1992.

Freeman, Roger A., *UK Airfields of the Ninth Air Force: Then and Now*, Battle of Britain Prints, 1994.

Hamlin, John F., *Support and Strike! A Concise History of the US Ninth Air Force in Europe*, G.M.S. Enterprises, 1991.

Hendrie, Andrew, *Short Sunderland in World War II*, Airlife, 1990.

Hockley-Farrar, Anthony, *The Army in the Air: The History of the Army Air Corps*, Alan Sutton, 1994.

Hough, Richard & Richards, Denis, *The Battle of Britain: The Jubilee History*, Hodder & Stoughton, 1989.

Legg, Rodney, *Dorset at War: Diary of WW2*, Dorset Pub. Co., 1990.
" " *Dorset Aviation Encyclopaedia*, Dorset Pub. Co., 1996.

McIntosh, Dave, *Terror in the Starboard Seat*, General Pub. Co. Ltd., Canada, 1980.

Mason, Francis K., *The Hawker Typhoon & Tempest*, Aston Publns., 1988.

Millgate, Helen D. (Editor), *Mr Brown's War: A Diary of the Second World War*, Alan Sutton, 1998.

Munson, Kenneth, *Flying Boats & Seaplanes since 1910*, Blandford Press, 1971.

Murray, Williamson, *The Luftwaffe, 1933–45*, Brassey's Inc. USA, 1996.

Phipp, Mike, *A History of Dorset & New Forest Airfields*, Mike Phipp, 1994.

Pomeroy, Colin A., *Military Dorset Today*, Silver Link Pub. Ltd., 1995.

Price, Alfred, *Battle of Britain Day*, Sidgwick & Jackson, 1990.
" " *The Hardest Day*, Macdonald, 1979.

Ramsey, W. G. (Ed), *The Battle of Britain: Then and Now*, Battle of Britain Prints, 1980.

Rawlings, John, *Fighter Squadrons of the RAF and their Aircraft*, Crecy Books, 1993.

Richards, Denis & Sanders, H., *The Royal Air Force, 1939–45*, HMSO, 1953.

Rust, Kenn C., *The 9th Air Force in World War II*, Aero Publishers, USA, 1970.

Shores, Christopher F., *2nd Tactical Air Force*, Osprey, 1970.

Smith, David J., *Britain's Military Airfields, 1939–45*, PSL 1989.

Taylor, H. A., *Airspeed Aircraft since 1931*, Putnam, 1971.

Terraine, John, *The Right of the Line*, Hodder & Stoughton, 1985.

Webb, Edwin & Duncan, John, *Blitz over Britain*, Spearmount Ltd, 1990.

White, A., *Christchurch Airfield*, A. White, 1987.
Wood, Derek & Dempster, Derek, *The Narrow Margin*, Hutchinson, 1961.
Wynn, Kenneth G., *Men of the Battle of Britain*, Gliddon Books, 1989.
Ziegler, Frank H., *The Story of 609 Squadron: Under the White Rose*, Crecy Books, 1971.

Index

Squadrons

USAAF